Studies in
Writing & Rhetoric

IN 1980, THE CONFERENCE ON COLLEGE COMPOSITION AND COM-
munication perceived a need for providing publishing opportunities
for monographs that were too long for publication in its journal and
too short for the typical scholarly books published by The National
Council of Teachers of English. The Studies in Writing and Rhetoric
series was conceived, and a Publications Committee established.

Monographs to be considered for publication may be speculative,
theoretical, historical, analytical, or empirical studies; research reports; or other works contributing to a better understanding of composition and communication, including interdisciplinary studies or
studies in related disciplines. The SWR series will exclude textbooks,
unrevised dissertations, book-length manuscripts, course syllabi,
lesson plans, and collections of previously published material.

Any teacher-writer interested in submitting a work for publication in this series should submit either a prospectus and sample
manuscript or a full manuscript to the NCTE Director of Publications, 1111 Kenyon Road, Urbana, IL 61801. Accompanied by sample
manuscript, a prospectus should contain a rationale, a definition of
readership within the CCCC constituency, comparison with related
extant publications, a tentative table of contents, and an estimate of
length in double-spaced 8½ × 11 sheets and the date by which full
manuscript can be expected. Manuscripts should be in the range of
100 to 170 typed manuscript pages.

The present work serves as a model for future SWR monographs.

Paul O'Dea
NCTE Director of Publications

Writing Instruction in Nineteenth-Century American Colleges

James A. Berlin

WITH A FOREWORD BY DONALD C. STEWART

Published for Conference on College
Composition and Communication

SOUTHERN ILLINOIS UNIVERSITY PRESS
Carbondale and Edwardsville

Production of works in this series has been partly funded by the Conference on College Composition and Communication of the National Council of Teachers of English.

Printed in the United States of America
Designed by Design for Publishing, Inc., Bob Nance
Production supervised by Kathy Giencke

Library of Congress Cataloging in Publication Data

Berlin, James A.
  Writing instruction in nineteenth-century
American colleges.

  (Studies in writing and rhetoric)
  Bibliography: p.
  1. English language—Rhetoric—Study and teaching—
United States—History.   2. Education, Higher—United
States—History—19th century.   I. Title.   II. Series:
Studies in writing & rhetoric.
PE1405.U6B47   1984   808'.042'071173   83-20116
ISBN 0-8093-1166-6

93 92 91   5 4 3

To My Parents

Contents

Foreword
Donald C. Stewart

IT IS THE MARK OF EDUCATED PERSONS TO ASK THEMSELVES, CON-
stantly, "Why do we think the way we do?" It is the mark of educated teachers of English composition to ask themselves, constantly,
"Why do we teach what we teach? What aspects of English composition are more important than others? Why do we think they are
more important?" Many teachers of English composition could not
answer these questions very well because (1) they have never asked
them of themselves, and (2) even if they have asked them, they lack
the historical knowledge necessary for significant answers.

For this reason, James Berlin's monograph takes on special significance. It joins an astonishingly small list of works of serious scholar-
ship which attempt to give teachers of English composition a sense
of history about the one course which has, for decades, been taken
by more American college students than any other.

We find here an analysis of the epistemological assumptions underlying classical, psychological-epistemological, and romantic rhetoric,
each, in its time, argues Berlin, accepted because of its compatibility with the prevailing mood and temperament of a particular era.
He concludes with an analysis not only of current-traditional rhetoric, essentially that inherited from the late nineteenth century, but
of what he chooses to call "expressionism" and "the new rhetoric."
The latter term embraces the virtues of expressionist rhetoric's concern for the integrity of the writer's self and classical rhetoric's
concern for language in a social context.

Berlin's monograph, as he would be the first to admit, is not a definitive statement on nineteenth-century rhetoric. But it is a thor-

oughly researched and thoughtful treatment of the subject, a significant contribution to a developing discussion of the rhetoric of this period and its implications for modern pedagogy. It is the kind of document that makes possible a definitive study of the subject and the period.

Equally important, in my judgment, is the philosophical seriousness of this work. Its author is not content with giving us this history of the ideas which have dominated rhetoric and composition instruction for a century and a half; nor is he content to point out the necessity of understanding the epistemological assumptions which have governed the particular rhetorics during this era. He has taken us one giant step further when he says, in his conclusion, that "the way we teach writing behavior, whether we will it or not, causes reverberations in all features of a student's private and social behavior. . . . in teaching students about the way they ought to use language we are teaching them something about how to conduct their lives." That is, I believe, as solid a justification for the teaching of composition as one will find anywhere.

Manhattan, Kansas
August 1983

Acknowledgments

I WOULD LIKE TO THANK THE NATIONAL ENDOWMENT FOR THE Humanities for providing two occasions to work on this manuscript: a fellowship in residence for college teachers in 1978–79 and a summer seminar for college teachers in 1980. Gratitude is also due the Taft Committee of the University of Cincinnati for a summer grant in 1983 that enabled me to complete the project.

Paul O'Dea and the Publications Committee for Studies in Writing and Rhetoric deserve thanks for being patient and helpful throughout, especially the two anonymous Committee members who took the pains to write a detailed critique of the first draft.

I also wish to express heartfelt thanks to Robert Arner, Judith Remy Leder, and Nuha Nasrallah for their generous support. Finally, gratitude too deep for words goes to the patience and inspiration offered by my wife Sam and my sons Dan and Christopher.

Writing Instruction in Nineteenth-Century American Colleges

1

The Method and the Major Theories

A RHETORIC IS A SOCIAL INVENTION. IT ARISES OUT OF A TIME and place, a peculiar social context, establishing for a period the conditions that make a peculiar kind of communication possible, and then it is altered or replaced by another scheme. A rhetoric is the codification of the unspeakable, as well as the speakable. No rhetoric—not Plato's or Aristotle's or Quintilian's or Perelman's—is permanent, is embraced by all people, or even by some one person or group, at all times. A rhetoric changes in the same way that a poetic changes, responding to the same social conditions. The study of rhetoric is made difficult, as well as enticing, by this inevitability.[1] In any social context, furthermore, there are usually a number of rhetorics competing for allegiance. A glance at any of the standard rhetorical histories—Kennedy's, McKeon's, Howell's, Corbett's—reveals this plurality of systems, each one claiming to be the one, true, and permanent.

In examining rhetoric in nineteenth-century American colleges, this flux and this diversity are striking throughout. In fact, for most of the century, three distinct conceptions of rhetoric vie for dominance, one of them split into two branches. Before considering these developments, I would like to explore the reasons behind rhetoric's disposition to change and conflict.

Rhetoric has traditionally been seen as based on four elements interacting with each other: reality, writer or speaker, audience, and language. Rhetorical schemes differ from each other, I am convinced, not in emphasizing one of these elements over another. Rhetorical schemes differ in the way each element is defined, as well as in the conception of the relation of the elements to each other. Every rhetoric, as a result, has at its base a conception of reality, of human nature, and of language. In other terms, it is grounded in a noetic field: a closed system defining what can, and cannot, be known; the nature of the knower; the nature of the relationship between the knower, the known, and the audience; and the nature of language.[2] Rhetoric is thus ultimately implicated in all a society attempts. It is at the center of a culture's activities.

Rhetoric thus has important consequences for the way people behave. When freshmen learn to write or speak, they are learning more than how to perform an instrumental task, useful in getting through college and in preparing for professional life. They are learning assumptions about what is real and what is illusory, how to know one from the other, how to communicate the real, given the strengths and limitations of human nature, and finally, how language works. In the composition or communications class, the student is being indoctrinated in a basic epistemology, usually the one held by society's dominant class, the group with the most power. Because writing and speech teachers are thus given a large responsibility, it is understandable that the rhetoric course has been through history the center of a student's education. It is more difficult to grasp why rhetoric courses since the late nineteenth century have fallen from favor, despite the fact that they often remain among the only required courses in an otherwise elective curriculum. The answer to this perplexing situation can be found, I am convinced, in examining the noetic fields underlying the rhetorics taught in these classrooms, and considering their place in larger social structures. This will be one concern of my study.

On a smaller scale, the noetic field underlying a particular rhetoric determines how the composing process is conceived and taught in the classroom. What goes into the process—the way in which invention, arrangement, and style are undertaken, or not undertaken, as is sometimes the case—is determined by the assumptions made, and often unexamined, about reality, writer/speaker, audience, and language. Each rhetoric, therefore, indicates the behavior appropriate to the composing situation. Beyond that, it directs the behavior of teacher and student in the classroom, making certain kinds of activity inevitable and other kinds impossible. In a time like the present one, examples of two different rhetorics, each defining the composing process in a different way and leading to patterns of behavior totally at odds with each other, within the classroom and without, can sometimes be seen on a single campus. The significance of this is that the behavior the student is told to undertake in composing leads to his embracing the tacit noetic field underlying it, whether or not teacher and student are aware of the fact (and they often are not). An examination of the relation between pedagogy and noetic fields will be a second concern of this study.

Given the central role of rhetoric in a society, it is understandable that the field of rhetoric is as pluralistic as society itself, despite the attempts of dictators, totalitarian states, and other tyrannies to create a simple, monolithic system. The rhetorics of a society are, furthermore, a useful index to the competing noetic fields found in that society. Rhetorics arise, fall, or alter in accordance with the conditions that make for change in society as a whole. They are engaging in themselves, but, because they are sensitive indicators of the extent of change in society, they are also a useful index of larger social developments. Thus, studying a rhetoric in its relationship to society reveals a great deal about both a rhetoric and the society producing it.

In discussing the rhetorics of American colleges in the nineteenth century, I will be identifying the noetic field that underlies each, and the implications of it for the teaching of writing and speaking, but especially writing. I will also be glancing at the social conditions that make for the existence of these competing fields. I want to emphasize at the start that I do not intend a simple chronicle of developments. My study is interpretive, attempting to make sense out of the multiplicity of theories, practices, textbooks, and the like found in the nineteenth century. In arriving at my interpretation, I have been especially indebted to two groundbreaking studies: Warren Guthrie's series of articles in *Speech Monographs*, entitled "The Development of Rhetorical Theory in America, 1635–1850," and Albert Kitzhaber's 1953 dissertation, "Rhetoric in American Colleges 1850–1900." Both are intelligent and accurate introductions to nineteenth-century rhetoric, deserving more attention from English teachers than they have received.[3]

The nineteenth century displays three distinct rhetorical systems that must be considered, although only two remain in force at the end of the century. The first is classical in origin, deriving from Aristotle, Cicero, and Quintilian. The second is psychologicalespistemological rhetoric (Douglas Ehninger's term), which I will refer to as eighteenth-century rhetoric. The third is romantic rhetoric, growing out of the transcendental movement and in most ways uniquely American in its development. Each of these rhetorics is based on a noetic field—a notion of reality, interlocutor, audience, and language—that makes for a distinctive view of the composing process, dictating unique behavior for the composer and for the teacher and student who are studying the composing process. Each of these fields also indicates an important relationship between what is going on in the classroom and what is happening in the larger society.

The Three Rhetorics

The classical approach to teaching writing was all but moribund in America at the beginning of the nineteenth century, despite its dominance in the previous century. John Quincy Adams' *Lectures on Rhetoric and Oratory*, a statement of classical rhetoric published in 1810, was, for example, without influence even in its own time. Still, classical rhetoric must be understood in order to realize the radical transformation that rhetorical systems undergo in nineteenth-century America. This rhetoric, furthermore, provides the most comprehensive view of the discipline ever devised, as well as the language generally used to discuss it.

Classical rhetoric defines the real as rational.[4] The universe is governed by the rules of reason, and the human mind is so constructed that, at its best, it is governed by the same rules. Knowledge is therefore found through the formulization of these rules of reason—in Aristotelian logic. This logic is deductive, requiring the application of generalizations to particular situations—in other words, the use of the syllogism. Induction is included in the system, but it is not as important as deduction because truth must always be derived through a set of prior, nonempirical principles, found through the rules of deductive logic, that will explain the significance of the particular.

For Aristotle, the realm of dialectic, of learned discourse, is governed by this strict, logical mode of thinking. Aristotle recognized, however, that the rules governing learned discourse did not apply to other areas of discourse. Although dialectic lends itself to logical discussion, because it deals with philosophical and scientific matters existing at a high level of probability, Aristotle realized there are other, equally important, but much less certain areas of human concern. This is the realm of rhetoric. As Perelman and Olbrechts-Tyteca have indicated, Aristotle was attempting to establish in his rhetoric a method for arriving at truth that was as compelling—however different—as was logic in the realm of dialectic.[5] Rhetoric thus deals with the probable, the uncertain and mutational world of discourse in the courts, in the legislature, and in other public assemblies.

Aristotle always considers rational truth to be the most important object of human discourse. Yet he recognized that, where rhetoric applies, other kinds of persuasion are equally compelling—indeed, should be compelling. Thus, the *Rhetoric* offers advice in preparing a speech that includes the emotional and ethical appeals, as well as the rational. The aim of rhetoric becomes the discovery of the available means of persuasion in these three areas—areas that correspond to the elements of consciousness.

The main concern of Aristotle's rhetoric accordingly becomes invention, discovering the available means of persuasion in the three areas appropriate to human nature. Aristotle's notion of discovery is different from our own. Since his rhetoric is deductive, the search for the available means of persuasion amounts to exploring what one already knows, and then applying it to the situation under consideration. Aristotle would have his students study commonplaces appropriate to the rational, emotional, and the ethical appeals, always certain that their discoveries might be persuasive in new ways, but never original in the sense that new truths are offered. Aristotle's rhetoric thus tends to be conservative politically, relying as it does on a storehouse of knowledge that all educated people are presumed to possess. Indeed, this conservatism was partly responsible for its dominance from the Middle Ages through the eighteenth century.

In Aristotle, then, we discover a noetic field in which the world is made up of a finite set of truths, logically arranged and discovered through logical principles. The knower is attempting to act in conformance with the rules of reason. In communicating these rational truths in the rhetorical realm, in the area of popular discourse, however, the speaker realizes that individuals are swayed by appeals to emotion and appeals designed to establish the speaker's character. Ethics and aesthetics are grounded in the rational, but in practice involve the emotional, and Aristotle accepts this as inevitable, taking it into account in his rhetoric.

Language for Aristotle is little more than a simple sign system, with thought and word enjoying a separate existence, to be brought together only for purposes of communication. Rational truths exist apart from the means used to express them. It should also be mentioned that Aristotle's rhetoric is preeminently oral and politically conservative. It is oral, at least in part, because it is designed for speaking situations involving small groups. It is conservative in that these small groups usually comprise a ruling elite, established and maintained by a preexistent body of truths.

Classical rhetoric in American colleges was overthrown with English rule, partly because it was associated with English colleges and an English way of life, partly because it was grounded in a noetic field that was being repudiated everywhere, but nowhere with such fervor as in America. The new field likewise came from abroad, but this time from Scottish, not English, colleges. Americans in the nineteenth century embraced Scottish Common Sense Realism, a concept of human experience that proved uniquely compatible with American economic, religious, and even aesthetic experience.

Scottish Common Sense Realism locates reality in two discrete realms, the spiritual and the material, and posits a set of separate and likewise discrete mental faculties constituted so as to apprehend each. While the spiritual world is ultimately the most important—proponents of this school were most commonly Presbyterian clergymen—this is not the main focus of the philosophy. Each person has the faculty that enables him to perceive spiritual truths—specifically, Protestant Christian truths—but this realm is a matter of individual conscience, a pact between the person and his maker that cannot be defined from without. This same insistence on the primacy of using one's faculties unencumbered by the interpretations of others is found in the material realm. The world of sense data exists independently of us and can be apprehended by the use of our senses and our faculties. Reliance on the observations of others, especially those from the past, leads to distortion. It is the realm of sense data and the logic that arises out of it—the inductive logic of science—that concerns the Common Sense Realists and the rhetoricians who call upon them.

Common Sense Realism consciously rebels against Aristotelian philosophy. Reality is discovered through observation, in the use of the senses and the faculties without regard for traditional wisdom. Induction thus becomes the method for securing truth, and deduction is declared all but useless. In communicating, the individual matches up the sign with the idea —the impression (literally) sense data has made on the mind. Once again, truth is extralingual, existing apart from the arbitrary signs used to express it. In using language to communicate, furthermore, the speaker or writer (both are important) attempts to appeal to the faculties of the auditor, to reproduce through language the original experience in the observer. Hence, the importance of being specific and vivid.

The rhetorical treatises of George Campbell and Hugh Blair embrace this noetic field, eventually becoming—along with that of Richard Whately—the dominant rhetorics in America until the last three decades of the nineteenth century. While both Campbell and Blair embrace Common Sense Realism, each offers a rhetoric with a different emphasis, leading to two dominant but distinct developments in the teaching of rhetoric in the nineteenth century. When speaking of the features they share in common, I shall use the term "eighteenth-century rhetoric." George Campbell's *Philosophy of Rhetoric* (1776) and its offshoots will be called "psychological rhetoric." Hugh Blair's influence, stemming from his *Lectures on Rhetoric and Belles Lettres* (1783), will be indicated by the term "belletristic rhetoric."

Campbell attempted to ground rhetoric in human nature, making his treatise, in fact as well as name, a philosophical statement. Human nature for him comprises a mechanical system of faculties that have been made so as to correspond exactly with the material and spiritual realms. Different faculties are used for different experiences, the apotheosis of human endeavor in language on earth to be found in oratory, involving as it does all the faculties and their counterparts in the world. (Poetry, in fact, is in Campbell's scheme considered inferior to oratory.) Campbell is thus among the first to argue for forms of discourse: exposition appealing to the understanding; narration, description, and poetry to imagination; argumentation to reason; and persuasion to all of these, but especially to the emotions and the will.

Campbell's rhetoric emphasizes induction—the use of the faculties for direct observation—specifically attacking Aristotle's emphasis on deduction. It departs from Artistotle in other important ways.[6] Invention is taken out of the realm of rhetoric, being relegated to the methodology of the discipline involved—most commonly, the scientific method—or to genius, as in the case of poetry and oratory. Aristotle's rational appeal is replaced by the appeal to experience, recording it exactly as it transpired, in all its vivid specificity. Obviously, no inventional devices are needed here. The ethical, the appeal from character, is likewise ignored. The emotional appeal is important to Campbell, however, securing as it does the assent of the will, the source of all human action. This discussion of emotion, however, is made an element of style, not invention. Rhetoric becomes concerned with adapting the message to the faculties of the audience. The effects of this position on arrangement are only implied in Campbell, but its implications for style are specific. Language and thing are considered separate, but the discussion of style—perspicuity, energy, vivacity, and the like—becomes central because of the importance of language in reproducing the content of experience in the minds of the audience.

As we shall see, the psychological rhetorics produced by Americans emulating Campbell—Henry Day, M. B. Hope, and John Bascom, for example—preserve the philosophical basis of the original, trying to ground their statements in human nature and emphasizing the forms of discourse and style.

Hugh Blair's treatise is based on the same noetic field as that of Campbell. Blair, however, emphasizes style almost (but not quite) exclusively. He argues that if the student learns to appreciate literature—to master the principles of literary criticism—he will have mastered the principles needed to produce a text. Reading, in other words, inevitably leads to efficient writing. Blair thus offers the application of aesthetic principles to literature. It must be noted, however, that his aesthetic is eighteenth-century and mechanistic. Art is conceived within the commonplace tradition, expressing "What oft was thought, but ne'er so well expressed," to use Pope's formulation.[7] The elements of a metaphor, for example, are considered mechanically and artificially joined, designed for pleasure, not truth value, and easily translated and explained in discursive prose. Blair, like Campbell, accordingly sees rhetoric as the study of all discourse —historic, philosophic, poetic, and oratorical. But in teaching students to produce a text, he argues, rhetoric can deal only with stylistic principles as found in literary works. Invention is specifically declared outside of rhetoric, and arrangement is hardly considered at all. Finally, Blair underscores rhetoric as being concerned with written rather than oral discourse, in emphasis if not in direct statement.

The new rhetoric of the eighteenth century was wholeheartedly embraced by Americans in the nineteenth century. It was compatible with the materialistic bent of the economic expansion taking place in the country, with its emphasis on technology. It was compatible with the dominant American literary theory of the mid-century. Finally, since it included traditional Protestant doctrine without imposing dogma, it was amenable to the religious diversity of the age.

Eighteenth-century rhetoric was eventually modified at the end of the nineteenth century to become the dominant paradigm for composition instruction in American colleges of the twentieth century. In the eighties and nineties, the elective system at the new American university—based, itself, on a faculty psychology—divided the entire academic community into discrete parts, leading to an assembly-line conception of education. As far as rhetoric is concerned, this meant that persuasive discourse—the appeal to the emotions and the will—was now seen to be possible only in oratory, and concern for it was thus relegated to the speech department. Discourse dealing with imagination was made the concern of the newly developed literature department. The writing course was left to attend to the understanding and reason, deprived of all but the barest emotional content. Encouraged by the business community, with the tacit approval of science departments, composition courses became positivistic in spirit and method.

Romantic rhetoric did not find its way into composition courses until late in the century, despite the fact that it grew out of the work of such important figures as Emerson, Thoreau, and others involved in the transcendental movement. Their impact, furthermore, for all of their strength in other areas, was almost completely ignored in college textbooks until late in the century. Yet romantic rhetoric was a significant force that must be considered.

Romantic rhetoric places the composing process, the act of writing and speaking, at the center of knowing. Reality is located not in the external world, the realm of the senses and the perceptive faculties, but in the interaction of observer and observed. A faculty psychology is employed, but it is conceived in completely different dimensions. The material world is looked upon as being informed with an ideal element, an underlying reality that is discovered only through an act of interpretation brought to experience by the observer. The facts of science are of limited value because by themselves they are essentially inhuman, including as they do only a part of human nature. The fully functioning individual constructs reality through synthesizing all of the faculties, the spiritual as well as the corporeal, in an act of creation. Reality is a construct which brings the ideas of the higher faculties into contact with the impressions of sense data, revealing the true significance of the material and the ideal in the larger scheme of nature. What we find in experience, therefore, is a function of what we bring to the experience as well as what is brought to us, and, unlike the Aristotelians, the ideas we bring to bear on any experience are not necessarily grounded in the rational. They instead involve a holistic response, engaging all the faculties—rational, moral, aesthetic—and they arrive at meaning through synthesis of all parts of human nature.

In composing—writing or speaking—the interlocutor must be certain that he is bringing all his faculties—all of his ideas and all relevant sense data—to the issue at hand. He must respond not as a scientist or Christian or even as an artist (although the best art includes the complete response), but as a fully functioning human being. The audience is an important part of composing, since the individuals comprising it must be appealed to on all levels of their being. For this reason, romantic rhetoric commonly considers oratory superior to written communication, primarily because it uses all features of consciousness, sensory—the voice, the body—as well as the intellectual. It is also possible for the orator to respond to the audience as the presentation is made, creating a dialectic of speaker and listener that corresponds to the dialectic of subject and object. Thus, romantic rhetoric converges with eighteenth-century rhetoric in valuing oral above written discourse, while denying the validity of its predecessor.

Romantic rhetoric gives rise to a conception of language that is as

revolutionary in the nineteenth century as the noetic field it pro-
poses. While the signs that make up language are conceived as arbitrary, the relation between signifier and signified is not. Because
the terms that comprise language are a part of the material realm,
they can only signify objects in the material world. Reality, however, transcends the merely physical, including the ideal, the realm
of ideas that individuals bring to their experience of the material
and that must inform it. The problem is to find a way of expressing
through language what itself transcends language. By the use of the
analogical method, the individual can suggest what exists beyond
language. Metaphor can express the unity of the ideal and the material, suggesting realms of being that are beyond the counters of
physical existence. The tenor and vehicle of a metaphor are not mechanically merged for purposes of providing mere pleasure. This fusion, instead, creates a meaning that embodies ultimate reality, a
meaning inexpressible in any other way. To separate the elements of
a metaphor is to destroy meaning: the meaning is the metaphor.
Furthermore, there is a premium placed on originality in the creation of metaphors, since the continuous use of them tends to destroy their ability to suggest what is beyond the mere material, making them a part of the material world.

Romantic rhetoric finds its way into composition classrooms in the
work of Fred Newton Scott, Joseph Villiers Denney, and Gertrude
Buck in the last decade of the century and later, although in a somewhat attenuated form. Still, for a time, it exerts a force that, although eventually defeated at the college level, is a continous presence in public elementary and secondary schools throughout the
twentieth century. It is eventually restored to the college level later
in the twentieth century, and its implications are explored to create
a new species of rhetoric.

In the chapters that follow, I will explore these three rhetorics in
greater detail. I am especially concerned with their implications for
the kinds of behavior that take place in the classroom—the ways in
which each dictates particular activities for student and teacher.
This classroom performance is in turn related to the larger purposes
of the university, which leads me to an exploration of each rhetoric—especially its pedagogy—in the context of the society that creates it.

I should mention one other caveat before proceeding. I will be

trying to give each rhetoric considered a fair hearing, although it
will be impossible for me to conceal my bias against eighteenth-
century rhetoric and my predilection for romantic rhetoric. I hope
to avoid overstating my preference by attending to the social conditions that made one kind of rhetoric impossible and another kind
inevitable. Along the same lines, I will also attempt to avoid the
temptation to see the nineteenth century as a testing ground for
rhetorics to be embraced by the present time. Nineteenth-century
rhetoricians were not trying to make rhetorics for us, and ought not
to be faulted for not having done so. Having said all this, I should
add that I plan to comment briefly on twentieth-century writing instruction in the final chapter of this study.

2

The Demise of the Classical Tradition

DESPITE THE IMPORTANCE OF THE RHETORIC OF RAMUS IN AMERica in the seventeenth century, classical rhetoric had remained alive, becoming dominant in the eighteenth century. The early popularity of Ramus, which encouraged a stylistic rhetoric of ornamentation, was due to the Puritan influence in higher education. As Guthrie points out, "Rhetoric to the colonists before 1730 is predominantly the art of ornamenting speech, and its parts are *elocutio* and *pronuntiatio*."[1] Ramus was associated with disestablished religious sects, those outside the ruling structures of church and state. He had, in fact, proposed his rhetoric in opposition to Aristotle, who represented the Scholastic tradition embodied in European universities. The restoring of classical rhetoric to the commanding position in the curriculum brought American colleges back in line with English universities. The reasons were in large part economic; colonists discovered that their material welfare was inextricably connected with that of their homeland. As a result, the impulse in American colleges between 1730 and the Revolution was to reestablish the English tradition of higher education. For rhetorical instruction, this meant a shift in thinking, moving from rhetoric as ornament to rhetoric as persuasion. The comprehensiveness of classical rhetoric was again established. Paradoxically, this scheme was used to address issues that would eventually lead to the separation of the colonies from England. The fact that classical rhetoric was so closely aligned with the government now overthrown, however, contributed to its inevitable decline, although this was not the only reason it was replaced.

As Ronald F. Reid indicates, "The latter part of the eighteenth century saw a profound change in American University education: the system of class tutors was replaced by one in which each tutor specialized in an academic field."[2] This represents one of the first changes in the American college, an early attempt to de-anglicize an important American institution. It also stands as the initial movement toward the specialization of both curriculum and faculty that was to reach its modern form in the elective system at Harvard under Eliot in the last two decades of the nineteenth century.

At first, however, the change at Harvard was formal only, the content of the curriculum remaining essentially the same as in the eighteenth century. Nicholas Boylston had provided 1,500 pounds for a chair of rhetoric at Harvard in 1771, but the endowment was not used until 1806, when John Quincy Adams was appointed the first Boylston Professor of Rhetoric. The statute of the endowment specifically stipulated that the instructor in rhetoric was to follow the classical model in theory and in classroom practice. This meant practically that the heads under which rhetoric was to be discussed had to be in keeping with the treatises of Aristotle, Cicero, Quintilian, or, at the least, one of their modern imitators. (John Ward's *A System of Oratory*, an English compendium of classical rhetoric, for example, was probably used as a model in drawing up the Boylston statutes.) Instruction was to focus on invention, disposition (arrangement), elocution (style), and pronunciation.

Before I turn to the content of such a program, it will be helpful to consider the behavior of teacher and student in the classroom, also explicitly stipulated by the statutes and typical of the time:

A committee of the Corporation prepared statutes which required the professor (1) to meet the freshman twice a week to discuss a classical text, portions of which students were to recite in English; (2) to meet the sophomores twice a week, devoting the first half-year to studying an English text, portions of which students were to recite from memory, and the second half to student delivery of non-original dialogues, speeches, and declamations and the writing of translations and original compositions; (3) to meet the juniors fortnightly to instruct from the English text started the previous year and to correct written compositions; (4) to meet the seniors fortnightly to correct written compositions; (5) to assist students who were to speak at public exhibitions; (6) to deliver weekly public lectures to the two upper classes and resident graduates; (7) to preside at weekly declamations of the two upper classes.[3]

Clearly, the exclusive duty of the college teacher was to teach. Students were also expected to study in certain prescribed ways. There was a strong emphasis on memorizing and translating both rhetorical theory contained in classical texts and models of effective speeches and literary works of the ancients. As the statutes summarized above indicate, there was also much practice in speaking and writing. It should be noted, however, that, in the words of Frederick Rudolph, there was "emphasis on teaching rather than on study; on students, rather than scholars; on order and discipline, rather than learning—all . . . derived from patterns which had been emerging in the residential colleges of the English universities."[4]

To observe the kind of rhetorical theory offered in such a classroom, it is only necessary to examine John Quincy Adams' *Lectures on Rhetoric and Oratory*, delivered between 1806 and 1809 and published in 1810. This rhetoric is comprehensive in every sense, leaving no part of the composing process to chance, offering explicit advice for the student at every step of the way. After announcing the scope of rhetoric—a version based on Aristotle, Cicero, and Quintilian—Adams presents nine lectures on invention, eight on arrangement, ten on style, one on delivery, and even one on memory. His deviation from his classical sources is minor. There are favorable references to Kames, Sheridan, and Walker, but in general his allusions to eighteenth-century English rhetorics are disparaging. And when he ignores the statutes, it is, as often as not, an attempt to expand the classical emphasis of the whole—the inclusion of memory, for example. In sum, while Adams departs from his classical sources at times—as will be seen—he is generally loyal to them.

At the outset, Adams makes clear that his noetic field is found in a rational universe populated by rational beings, conceived here in Christian terms:

> The peculiar and highest characteristic, which distinguishes man from the rest of the animal creation is REASON. It is by this attribute, that our species is constituted the great link between the physical and intellectual world. By our passions and appetites we are placed on a level with the herds of the forest; by our REASON we participate of the divine nature itself.[5]

The instrument of reason is language, making rhetoric the most significant study that humans can undertake:

> As the necessary adjunct and vehicle of reason, the faculty of speech was also bestowed as an exclusive privilege upon man; not the mere utterance of articulate sounds; not the mere cries of passion, which he has in common with the lower orders of animate nature; but as the conveyance of thought; as the means of rational intercourse with his fellow creature, and of humble communion with his God. It is by the means of reason, clothed with speech, that the most precious blessings of social life are communicated from man to man, and that supplication, thanksgiving, and praise, are addressed to the Author of the universe.[6]

The social importance of rhetoric is apparent, establishing the bonds that make for the welfare of the individual in his relations with others. The understanding and communication of experience is, furthermore, conceived in rational terms: "The connexion between genuine rhetoric and sound logic is indeed indissoluble. All good speaking must necessarily rest upon the basis of accurate thinking."[7] He goes on to argue that logic and rhetoric must be separated, but that they are closely related: "logic to the operations of the mind, within itself; rhetoric to the communication of their results to the minds of others." In this view, "logic is the store house, from which the instruments of rhetoric are to be drawn."[8]

Adams relies on this noetic field in discussing invention. He includes Aristotle's logical, ethical, and emotional appeals, providing students with devices for discovering the available means of persuasion—even though he conceives of rhetoric as including more than persuasion (scientific writing, for example). Aristotle is emphasized in the use of the enthymeme and example, including a discussion of the rational commonplaces, the questions to ask in probing a subject. His rational emphasis leads him to slight the emotional appeal, in decided departure from classical rhetoric, but he calls on Quintilian for the ethical appeal.[9] Adams also includes material from Cicero's discussion of topics and from Quintilian on generating matter in accordance with the purpose of the speech.[10]

Adam's discussion of the remaining offices of rhetoric represents a similar synthesis of Aristotle, Cicero, and Quintilian. His advice on the arrangement of the parts of a speech, for example, relies on

Cicero, and his treatment of style on Artistotle and Cicero. Quintilian and Cicero are the most important sources for his statement on delivery.[11]

As stated earlier, Adams' rhetoric is comprehensive, considering every feature of the composing process. He does depart from his classical sources in expanding the definition of rhetoric and in emphasizing reason at the expense of the emotional appeal. Part of the motivation for this divergence is that he is trying to apply classical rhetoric to a modern age. Adams is throughout aware that he is considering the role of rhetoric in a society that is different from that which gave rise to his models. He is, to echo the title of a well-known textbook from our own time, writing a classical rhetoric for the modern student.

Adams' rhetoric had little impact even in his own time. Initially published in 1810, it did not see another printing for 150 years.[12] It was so neglected that it was reviewed only three times following its appearance—fewer notices in print than it has had since 1950. Adams' rhetoric failed not because it was incompetent. It failed because it was no longer suited to the age. By the time it was printed, the rhetorics of Blair and Campbell had already begun to replace classical rhetoric at other colleges in America. The reasons for this demise of the classical system are not hard to find.

Adams' rhetoric was associated with an epistemology that was being assaulted on all fronts in America and abroad in the nineteenth century. For Aristotle, dialectic, the area of learned discourse, was governed by strict logical procedures. As I have already indicated, Artistotle's rhetoric—the model for Cicero and Quintilian—did not share this commitment to logic. Rhetoric was the realm of the emotional, and ethical as well, in discovering meaning, applicable whenever individuals communicated with each other about matters of law, legislation, and public virtue. These are areas outside of dialectic that, although dealing with the probable, are crucial to human experience. The nineteenth century revolted against Aristotelian logic as the means of arriving at truth in the area of learned discourse, or any other area for that matter. The new logic was empirical—a scientific logic. And in overthrowing Aristotelian logic, the age discarded Aristotelian rhetoric as well, if only for its association with the deductive method. Campbell's *Philosophy of Rhetoric* is explicit in establishing the link between deduction in logic and deduction in rhetoric, denying that any but the inductive method can be successful in either realm. As will be seen later, it is Campbell—not Aristotle, Cicero, or Quintilian—who serves as America's philosopher of rhetoric in the nineteenth century. The comprehensiveness, the flexibility, and the utility of classical rhetoric were lost, and probably for the wrong reason. This defeat is even more regrettable when we consider what is offered in the name of rhetoric at the end of the century.

This shift in epistemology—a basic change in the noetic field—did not occur in isolation, having its origins in economic realities. Classical rhetoric had been associated in America with the aristocratic universities of England throughout much of the seventeenth century and then again after the Revolution. For centuries it had served the needs of a society in which wealth and power were concentrated in the hands of a ruling class, a group that used the university to conserve its power. In other words, it was considered a feature of a conservative, monarchial political order. The basis of the curriculum was the literature of ancient Greece and Rome, which required the mastery of a language of learning that was deliberately made difficult of access for those outside the power structure.[13] The importance of deductive logic in classical rhetoric, the application of traditional wisdom to all experience, supported this world order. The college in America was intended for different purposes, even if it took considerable time to realize them. Aristocratic colleges ran counter to the American faith in democracy and in the importance of the self-made man of affairs. With the growth of the middle class, Americans came to value the practical and the scientific, not the literary in education. Even before the Revolution, science was making inroads in the curriculum of American colleges.[14] By the end of the nineteenth century, the classical idea of education had been completely defeated by the elective curriculum with its emphasis on the scientific method in all areas of study—even, as we shall see, in the traditional humanistic art of rhetoric.

3

The Triumph of Eighteenth-
Century Rhetoric

NINETEENTH-CENTURY THINKING ON RHETORIC IN AMERICA was completely dominated by Campbell, Blair, and Whately. Even when their works were no longer used in the classroom, after the Civil War, the paradigm that they established remained in force, providing the noetic field that underlies most statements about rhetoric. In this chapter I would like to look at the rhetoric of each, examining its details and the nature of its emphasis and subsequent influence. I also plan to comment on the compatibility of these rhetorics with American cultural patterns, especially since the happy marriage of British rhetoric and American culture is contrary to what we might expect.

Campbell

George Campbell published the *Philosophy of Rhetoric* in 1776, while serving as Principal of Marischal College, Aberdeen. He was attempting a new rhetoric that was to be the counterpart of the new logic. Campbell explores the implications of the speculation of Locke and Hume as they are interpreted in Scottish Common Sense Realism, developing a theory of communication grounded in a philosophy consciously opposed to Scholasticism. The Aristotelian world view, or Campbell's version of it, has been replaced by the Newtonian, and a new rhetoric is required. For Campbell, nature is an orderly mechanism, following ineluctable laws discoverable through the use of the mind. Reality, however, is no longer conceived as a rational construct revealing itself through the application of syllogistic logic. Campbell is quite specific on this point, devoting an entire chapter of the *Philosophy* to refuting the value of the syllogism, asserting that deductive logic can never discover truth in science or ethics, and, indeed, has only limited value in expressing the discoveries of induction. He finally dismisses the syllogism as the "schoolmen's science of defence," concluding:

> When all erudition consisted more in an acquaintance with words, and an address in using them, than in the knowledge of things, dexterity in this exercitation conferred as much lustre on the scholar, as agility in the tilts and tournaments added glory to the knight. In proportion as the attention of mankind has been drawn off to the study of nature, the honours of this contentious art have faded, and it is now almost forgotten. There is no reason to wish its revival, as eloquence seems to have been very little benefited by it, and philosophy still less.[1]

The "knowledge of things," the examination of nature through the inductive method, is central for Campbell. The mind is made up of a set of faculties that correspond perfectly to the experience provided by the material and spiritual world. Vincent Bevilacqua offers a helpful introduction to Campbell's philosophical sources:

> The common sense philosophers thus see the mind not as a *tabula rasa* void of everything but potential, but as an amalgam of powers, original senses, and propensities which afford immediate perception of self-evident truths. Their philosophical-epistemological position is between the rationalists and the empiricists, between Descartes and Hume. They maintain with the rationalists that there are senses of the mind prior to experience, but refuse to admit into their philosophy senses which are beyond observation. They hold with the empiricists that the true nature of the mind can be determined only by observation, but admit also original senses and propensities implanted in man by Nature and not derived from experience.[2]

This scheme enables Campbell, a clergyman and theologian, to advocate the inductive method in science as well as religion, calling upon the faculties of the mind, as posited by the Common Sense Realists, to function reliably in the spiritual and physical realms.

Given this epistemology, individuals communicate through using language to act on the faculties of the audience, attempting to reproduce the original experience in its entirety. As in Aristotle, language is divorced from the thing itself. The sign is an arbitrary device existing apart from meaning, the meaning being located in the sensory experience itself. Knowledge, in other words, is extralinguistic. Rhetoric then becomes an elaboration of how the mind of the auditor can be affected so as to reproduce the immediate experience of the interlocutor.

Campbell's rhetoric is often remarkably familiar, since it is the rhetorical system with which most writing and speech teachers are acquainted—however, unconciously. In looking at this system, it will also be helpful to keep in mind classical rhetoric, since Campbell is always conscious of the new directions he is establishing for rhetoric, given its historical development.

Campbell shifts the attention of rhetoric from invention, from the *discovery* of the available means of persuasion, to adapting the message, managing it, so as to affect the audience in the desired way: "In speaking there is always some end proposed, or some effect which the speaker intends to produce on the hearer. The word *eloquence* in its greatest latitude denotes, 'That art or talent by which the discourse is adapted to its end.'"[3] Campbell's reason for abandoning invention are obvious from what has already been said. A rhetoric that relies on induction for arriving at truth is not concerned with bringing appropriate arguments to bear on the issue at hand. Truth is discovered through careful observation. Deductive principles may prevent us from seeing the experience before us, causing distortion after the manner of Bacon's idols. The method for arriving at the content of discourse is thus outside of rhetoric's province. Rhetoric's concern is with shaping the message discovered outside the composing process so that it has the desired effect on the audience. Here, a knowledge of the faculties and their functions comes into play.

In a prefiguring of the "forms of discourse" that will later dominate the composition class in American colleges, Campbell discusses the ends of the rhetorical act and their relation to the faculties: "All the ends of speaking are reducible to four; every speech being intended to enlighten the understanding, to please the imagination, to move the passions, or to influence the will."[4] Campbell's focus on the psychological effects of rhetoric—rather than the invention of arguments—expands the scope of rhetoric, including communication of all kinds: legal, deliberative, ceremonial, historical, philosophical, scientific, and even poetic. Rhetoric thus becomes the study of how all discourse achieves its effects.

Campbell continually uses examples from poetry and drama to demonstrate his position, placing art at the center of his scheme. For Campbell, the loftiest expression of human art is found in oratory, exceeding even poetry in its possibilities. Behind this exaltation of oratory—specifically, persuasive oratory—is Campbell's concern with the faculties. Oratory simply engages more faculties in the speaker and the listener: the understanding, the imagination, the passions, the judgment, and the will. Thus, persuasive oratory transcends even poetry—the realm of imagination and passion—in its inclusiveness, becoming the apotheosis of human language acts.

This leads to another consideration. Despite his emphasis on induction, Campbell conceives of rhetoric as being primarily concerned with emotion. This again is linked to his view of persuasive oratory. Unlike the rhetoricians who will invoke him later in the nineteenth century, Campbell argues, "So far therefore it is from being an unfair method of persuasion to move the passions, that there is no persuasion without moving them." He goes on to explain:

> Let it be observed that, in order to persuade, there are two things which must be carefully studied by the orator. The first is, to excite some desire or passion in the hearers; the second is to satisfy their judgment that there is a connexion between the action to which he would persuade them, and the gratification of the desire or passion which he excites. This is the analysis of persuasion. The former is effected by communicating lively and glowing ideas of the object; the latter, unless so evident of itself as to supersede the necessity, by presenting the best and most forcible arguments which the nature of the subject admits. In the one lies the pathetic, in the other the argumentative. These incorporated together . . . constitute that vehemence of contention, to which the greatest exploits of eloquence ought doubtless to be ascribed.[5]

Campbell's use of such images as "lively and glowing" and "forcible" can be attributed to his mechanistic epistemology: the experience of attending to discourse must replicate the sensory experience of the material world. Beyond this, we can see that for Campbell both the rational and pathetic faculties must be aroused if persuasion is to take place, because persuasion always moves to action—otherwise it is not persuasion—and no motives are possible without emotion. Virtues, in fact, while not identical to emotions, are closely related to them: "They are, therefore, though not passions, so closely related to them, that they are properly considered as motives to action, being equally capable of giving an impulse to the will."[6] Finally, this emphasis on emotion makes sympathy, the identification of speaker and auditor, an important part of rhetoric.

The second and third parts of Campbell's *Philosophy* are devoted to the use of language. This discussion, as we shall see, follows inevitably from the theoretical first part. For Campbell, learning takes place in three ways, and only three ways: sensation, the direct experience of the material world; memory, the recollection of sensation; and imagination, the consciousness of what we do not directly know through sensation, or memory. The orator's task is to reproduce the effect of sensation, insofar as is possible, through concrete language. Hence derives the direction for using language that continues to appear in college textbooks on writing even today. As Campbell explains: "Eloquence hath always been considered, and very justly, as having a particular connexion with language. It is the intention of eloquence to convey our sentiments into the minds of others, in order to produce a certain effect upon them. Language is the only vehicle by which this conveyance can be made."[7]

In book 2, Campbell is concerned with usage, realizing that this is a matter of social custom, not rule. He discusses it under three heads: reputable use, national use, and present use. He also includes a long, four-part section on diction, and an entire chapter on "grammatical purity," centering on the barbarism, the solecism, and the impropriety: "The barbarism is an offence against etymology, the solecism against syntax, the impropriety against lexicography."[8] This section on usage grows out of a philosophical concern, as we have seen, but it is also, in part, a product of the interest of the new middle class in the social implications of language. This last consideration will make Campbell's discussion of usage central in American composition textbooks at the end of the nineteenth century.

At the start of chapter 5, in book 2, Campbell lists the qualities of style that he considers rhetorical rather than grammatical. These qualities—perspicuity, vivacity, elegance, animation, and music—are related to the faculties quite explicitly:

> But it is with the expression as with the sentiment, it is not enough to the orator that both be true. A sentence may be a just exhibition, according to the rules of the language, of the thought intended to be conveyed by it, and may therefore, to a mere grammarian, be unexceptionable; which to an orator may appear extremely faulty. It may, nevertheless, be obscure, it may be languid, it may be inelegant, it may be flat, it may be unmusical. It is not ultimately the justness either of the thought or of the expression, which is the aim of the orator; but it is a certain effect to be produced in the hearers. This effect as he purposeth to produce in them by means of language, which he makes the instruments of conveying his sentiments into their minds, he must take care in the first place that his style be perspicuous, that so he may be sure of being understood. If he would not only inform the understanding, but please the imagination, he must add the charms of vivacity and elegance, corresponding to the two sources from which, as was observed in the beginning of this work, the merit of an address of this kind results. By vivacity, resemblance is attained; by elegance, dignity of manner. For as to the dignity of the subject itself, or thing imitated, it concerns solely the thought. If he purposes to work upon the passions, his very diction, as well as his sentiments, must be animated. Thus language and thought, like body and soul, are made to correspond, and the qualities of the one exactly to cooperate with those of the other.[9]

It is not difficult to see in this statement a shift from Artistotle's concern for speaking the truth to a concern for gaining an effect. While Campbell would not have agreed with this implication, it is unavoidable, and will eventually take its toll in composition courses. The last statement, furthermore, explicitly offering Campbell's view of language, should be noted. The remainder of book 2 is concerned with perspicuity and all of book 3 with vivacity. Campbell never provided comments on the remaining qualities, but, it should be remembered, what he did offer grows consciously and inevitably out of his epistemology; it does not pretend to be a statement of isolated, self-evident principles, as will be the case in the late nineteenth century.

Blair

While Campbell's treatise was widely used in American colleges, the most popular treatment of rhetoric until after the Civil War was Blair's *Lectures on Rhetoric and Belles Lettres*. Blair's work went through 130 editions in England and America after being published in 1783, the last appearing in 1911. Like Campbell, Blair was a Scottish clergyman and teacher, serving as Regius Professor of Rhetoric and Belles Lettres at Edinburgh during the time the lectures were delivered. Both Campbell and Blair were commonly used together in America, not surprising when it is considered that they are grounded in a common noetic field. Blair also argues that the principles of rhetoric grow out of the principles of human nature, calling upon Scottish Common Sense Realism for his philosophical base. The important difference between the two is that Blair is intended to be a practical guide for students, not in any sense a theoretical text. More important, Blair focuses on the principles of literary taste, offering a textbook in literary analysis. His basic assumption is that effective writing is learned through studying examples of effective writing. The student must first learn the principles of expression before he can express himself. This belletristic bias appeals to the need Americans felt to develop a national literature, a unique American poetic voice. Furthermore, as Ehninger and Golden have pointed out, Blair was often read as a pre-romantic, a figure arguing for an aesthetic that sounds like the idealist position found in Emerson, Poe, and others.[10] In fact, Blair's literary theory is in every sense an eighteenth-century product, grounded in a positivist epistemology, a faculty psychology, and a mechanistic view of language. To read Blair as a romantic is to make romanticism compatible with eighteenth-century aesthetics, distorting romanticism's truly revolutionary character.

Blair's rhetoric is almost exclusively stylistic, concentrating on the effects of literature. He contradicts the comprehensiveness of classical rhetoric, specifically denying the possibility that the topics, or any other devices, can aid in invention. In discussing the offices of rhetoric, he says: "The first of these, Invention, is, without doubt, the most material, and the ground-work of the rest. But, with respect to this, I am afraid it is beyond the power of art to give any real assistance. Art cannot go so far, as to supply a speaker with arguments on every cause, and every subject; though it may be of considerable use in assisting him to arrange, and express those, which his knowledge of the subject has discovered."[11] Invention, relying again on the inductive observation of truth through the use of the faculties, "comes from a thorough knowledge of the subject, and profound meditation on it."[12] Discovery is relegated to direct observation, or, as is the case in art, to genius, about which I will add more in a moment.

The first half of this treatise reveals this plan for rhetoric. Significantly, Blair focuses on written rather than oral discourse, even though he seems to share Campbell's enthronement of persuasive oratory. After discussing the sources of literary taste, including the taste for the sublime, Blair devotes two chapters to the "Rise and Progress of Language" as well as writing. He follows this with two chapters on the structure of language, a chapter on perspicuity and precision in style, three on the structure of sentences, and four on figurative language. His discussion of the general features of style includes a chapter entitled "Diffuse, Concise—Feeble, Nervous—Dry, Plain, Neat, Elegant, Flowery" and one entitled "General Characters of Style—Simple, Affected, Vehement—Directions for forming a proper Style," both of which were to prove influential in later rhetorics. The first volume closes with five chapters applying these principles to eighteenth-century prose.

The first 10 chapters of volume 2 turn to oratory, but the last 13 return to written language, offering a scheme for classifying the branches of rhetoric as well as literature. Chapters one and two take up the history of oratory and three through five discuss the kinds of oratory—popular assemblies, the bar, and the pulpit. After devoting two chapters to the parts of a discourse, Blair gives a chapter to delivery and improving in oratory, here denying the role of invention in rhetoric. Having paid the obligatory attention to traditional rhetorical concerns, he returns to a discussion of writing. Here the expanded scope of rhetoric is underscored. Two chapters are given to historical writing, two to philosophical writing, and finally ten to poetry. He divides poetry into the pastoral, didactic, epic, and dramatic, providing examples of each.

Blair was important to nineteenth-century American rhetoric because he provided a model for using literature to teach writing. His literary theory is, however, in every way a product of the eighteenth century, concerned as it is with the effects of art on the audience.[13] This bias can be seen in his use of genius, perhaps the central concept in romanticism. Blair repeatedly emphasizes the role of genius in literature, making it the source of invention in poetry. He is not, however, speaking of the exalted, creative faculty of the romantics. As Blair explains, "It is used to signify that talent or aptitude which we receive from nature, for excelling in any one thing whatever. Thus we speak of a Genius for mathematics, as well as a Genius for poetry; of a Genius for war, for politics, or for any mechanical employment."[14] Likewise, the sublime in poetry is said to provide a powerful experience, arising out of nature as "the natural offspring of a strong imagination." The sublime, however, produces not a moment of vision unlocking the meaning of experience, but little more than "striking beauty in composition."[15]

It is true that Blair's definition of poetry in chapter 38 sounds remarkably like Coleridge in the *Biographia Literaria* or Wordsworth in the Preface to the *Lyrical Ballads*:

> The most just and comprehensive definition which, I think, can be given of poetry, is, "That it is the language of passion, or of enlivened imagination, formed, most commonly, into regular numbers." The Historian, the Orator, the Philosopher, address themselves for the most part, primarily to the understanding: their direct aim is to inform, to persuade, or to instruct. But the primary aim of a Poet is to please, and to move; and, therefore, it is to the Imagination, and the Passions, that he speaks. He may, and he ought to have it in his view, to instruct, and to reform; but it is indirectly, and by pleasing and moving, that he accomplishes this end. His mind is supposed to be animated by some interesting object which fires his Imagination, or engages his Passions; and which, of course, communicates to his Style a peculiar elevation suited to his ideas; very different from that mode of expression, which is natural to the mind in its calm, ordinary state.[16]

This constitutes a departure from the main thrust of Blair's conception of poetry, however, since in the same chapter he adds that it is the effect on the audience that distinguishes poetic statement. Poetry has now become, he explains, "a separate art, calculated chiefly to please, and confined generally to such subjects as related to the imagination and passions."[17]

To use M. H. Abrams' distinction, Blair's conception of poetry remains a matter of mirroring forth what is available to common observation.[18] The poet simply represents what his senses and faculties have discovered, couching it in an elevated style. Blair is solidly in the commonplace tradition, seeing poetry as "What oft was thought, but ne'er so well expressed." The poet does not create the forms of reality, but simply copies them. Thus, Blair explains, "All the qualities of a good Style may be ranged under two heads, Perspicuity and Ornament. For all that can possibly be required of Language, is, to convey our ideas clearly to the minds of others, and, at the same time, in such a dress, as by pleasing and interesting them, shall most effectually strengthen the impressions which we seek to make."[19] Likewise, in his chapter on figurative language, Blair repeatedly reveals his limited, mechanistic conception of language. Figures, he explains, increase our store of expression, bestow dignity (especially in poetry), provide the pleasure of comparison, make the abstract concrete, and heighten emotional effects. The only function of figures—the main element of poetry—is to present in a striking fashion that which is evident to the careful observer: "Not content with a simple communication of ideas and thoughts, it [language] paints those ideas to the eye; it gives colouring and relievo [sic], even to the most abstract conceptions. In the figures which it uses, it sets mirrors before us, where we may behold objects, a second time, in their likeness."[20]

Whately

Richard Whately's *Elements of Rhetoric* was commonly used along with Blair and Campbell, despite the fact that, on the face of it, his conception of rhetoric is not compatible with theirs. Whately considered his rhetoric to be a revival of Aristotle, a return to the deductive method in rhetoric. A close look at his treatise reveals, however, that Whately was firmly entrenched in the noetic field of eighteenth-century rhetoric. His work can be characterized as an attempt to wed an adumbrated deductive logic, derived from Aristotle, with an empirical epistemology. Despite his use of deduction, for example, he accepts the importance of emotion in persuasion, adopting Campbell's and Blair's distinction between argument as an appeal to reason, and persuasion as an appeal to reason and emotion. The result was that he fully developed the implications of Campbell, providing a new scheme of invention to suit the new psychological rhetoric, replacing in the process the Aristotelian notion of invention. In addition, like Blair, Whately's foremost recommendation to American teachers is the practical nature of his work. Whately wrote his *Elements* while serving as the Principal of St. Alban's Hall, Oxford, intending it to be a guide for his students. (He later served as Archbishop of Dublin.) The work is a composition textbook—not a theoretical statement or even a commentary on literature—and his model of the composing process became highly influential.

As Douglas Ehninger convincingly argues, Whately approved Campbell's effort to deny rhetoric a method of investigation peculiar to its own domain.[21] Campbell had taken invention out of rhetoric, relegating it to the new logic of science, the method of a particular discipline (most commonly, the scientific), or, as in the case of poetry, to genius. Campbell had not specified, however, how what had been discovered outside of the composing process was to be used in the rhetorical act. Whately filled the gap by providing a new *inventio* of management to replace the classical *inventio* of discovery. Whately provides specific advice on how material appropriated elsewhere is to be managed in composition, offering a two-part scheme.

He first provides a classification of the forms rational arguments may take—here preserving the distinction between argumentation and persuasion—explaining the way these must be structured if they are to provide a reliable conclusion. The topics—cause to effect, and the like—as well as kinds of syllogism and probable and demonstrative arguments are presented here. He then offers advice on when these rational arguments are to be used, depending on such variables as who, for example, has the presumption in his favor. In dealing with persuasion, he discusses the nature of emotions and derives principles for the kinds of appeals these make possible, as well as directions on when they are to be used. The emphasis throughout is on the effective presentation, on making convincing or persuasive what has been discovered outside the composing act.

Whately's description of how the composing process is to be taught in the classroom is perhaps the most pervasive feature of his scheme in later writing textbooks. Whately's starting point is to assist the student in finding a subject for a theme. It should be engaging to the student, and should focus on something he knows, selected from the student's studies, from stimulating conversation with elders, or from everyday occurrences of interest. Even insignificant subjects are to be allowed if they are of interest to the learner. Since discovery is not considered a part of the teacher's responsibility, correctness and style, not content, are what count. After finding the subject, the student is to state "the proposition or propositions to be maintained, clearly, and in a suitable form." How this proposition is discovered is left unexplained. It must, however, avoid "entering on too wide a field of discussion, and introducing many propositions not sufficiently connected."[22] In short, the thesis must be narrowed and focused. Outlining is encouraged since it "will give a coherence to the Composition, a due *proportion* of its several parts, and a clear and easy arrangement of them."[23] (This is reminiscent of the later emphasis on unity, coherence, and emphasis.) The proposition is then worked up into an informal essay, the student using "a free, natural, and simple style,"[24] although not one suitable to a book-length effort. Correctness in the use of language is to be emphasized. Finally, Whately advises that the student will improve "if the teacher will, after pointing out any faults in the learner's exercise, and making him alter or re-write it, if necessary, then put before him a composition on the same subject written by *himself*, or by some approved writer."[25] As in Blair, studying the principles used in criticizing the finished product is assumed to be valuable in learning to create the product itself. Finally, it is difficult to avoid noting that this plan for teaching composing is the one still found most commonly in today's composition textbooks, some 150 years after its presentation.

Pedagogy

It is impossible to overestimate the popularity of these three treatises in the college classrooms of America before the Civil War. The American textbooks that replace them between 1850 and 1870, furthermore, were little more than imitations. Guthrie presents a useful summary of where and how the three were used in colleges in the first half of the century, a listing that need not be repeated here.[26] It is noteworthy, however, that the amount of speaking and writing required in the courses based on them was much less than might be expected, especially when we consider that college faculties were devoted to teaching, and teaching only. Instead of producing discourse, students were expected to memorize the rhetorical principles governing discourse as they were explicated in Campbell, Blair, Whately, or one of their imitators. Kitzhaber explains:

> The most prominent educational theory in American colleges up to 1870 was based on the ideal of mental discipline. The human mind was widely regarded as consisting of certain faculties or powers: the will, the feelings, the judgment, the imagination, etc. It was believed that these faculties could be exercised and strengthened in much the same way as muscles. Educators, therefore, saw their functions as twofold: to discipline and strengthen these separate faculties through drill and exercises; and secondarily to supply the student with a store of general principles in the light of which his trained faculties would, in later professional life, make needed particular applications. The best sort of education was that which offered the best opportunities for rigorous drill, and that which stressed generalizations thought to be universally useful. The curriculum that best suited this approach was the traditional one centered chiefly around mathematics and the classical languages. Most of the curriculum was required, and deviations from it were discouraged since it not only provided essential mental discipline but it also furnished the sort of generalized culture thought to be most valuable. Instruction was by recitation, a method calculated to strengthen the faculty of memory; the student often memorized the pages of his textbook and repeated them to his teacher verbatim. Questions from the student usually were not encouraged, since the teacher did not consider it a part of his responsibility to add anything of his own to the lesson.[27]

This pedagogy seems to have adapted the new faculty psychology to the old, deductive method, ingraining general principles in students that come from the new inductive rhetoric. Students did, however, prepare themes and declamations. After all, their college years were designed to prepare them for the traditional professions of the ministry, law, and medicine—the first two demanding much rhetorical skill. Students continued to deliver and publish commencement day theses, for example, and these display considerable accomplishment. The actual study of rhetoric, however, tended to be confined to memorizing abstract principles. Students were learning to write and speak because they were writing and speaking in informal debating societies, as well as in the classes requiring the translation of ancient texts.

We must also remember that until about 1850 an anti-intellectual atmosphere commonly prevailed on American campuses. As Rudolph explains, "Americans were on the whole much more impressed by the careers of self-taught, self-made men, men whose elevation to positions of responsibility, eminence, and wealth was accomplished without benefit of formal schooling. Against this record of success, the colleges could with difficulty advance the necessity of close, rigorous intellectual exercise as a justification for attending college. In the end, the colleges to a certain extent incorporated a posture of anti-intellectualism in their behavior."[28] This tendency was of course enhanced by the sectarian religious bias at many American colleges, where the devotion to God was more important than the devotion to learning. Finally, colleges tended to be elitist establishments at this time, places for the children of the well-to-do, young people who came to higher education with rhetorical skills that had been encouraged in their homes.

The Social Setting

Campbell, Blair, and Whately could become so overwhelmingly dominant in American colleges only because they were compatible with the social and intellectual climate of the time. From one point of view, this is puzzling. After all, the three were clerics and university teachers who supported established religious, political, and social arrangements quite different from those found in America. Their popularity seems to have been the result of their not being altogether incompatible with the American belief in individualism, equality, and self-government. Of equal importance, they were congenial to American predispositions in philosophy, religion, and art.[29]

The dominant philosophy in America in the first half of the nineteenth century was Scottish Common Sense Realism, primarily as found in the work of Thomas Reid, James Beattie, Dugald Stewart, and Thomas Brown.[30] (We have already seen the central place of this thought in Campbell and Blair.) The large number of Scottish immigrants in America had something to do with this preference. More important, this philosophy offered the Protestant clergymen who dominated American colleges during this time an antidote to the atheism and materialism of Hume and Voltaire, on the one hand, and a refuge from the philosophical perplexities of Berkeley and his German counterparts, on the other.[31] It further offered a bland Christian doctrine that did not upset the delicate balance of competing religious sects. And while it served God, it also provided adequately for mammon. Its empiricism did not interfere with a free economy which relied on scientific technology. Finally, the emphasis on common sense seemed to support the democratic glorification of the common person, endowed by God with faculties that gave him freedom and dignity. In other words, Common Sense Realism was safe, politically and religiously.

Americans were eager to establish a national art, uniquely expressive of the American experience, at this time. The allegiance to English models had not yet been defeated, however. Blair's rhetoric, with its belletristic emphasis, was especially appealing. The aesthetic that guided American literary criticism in America until about 1835 was eighteenth-century and English in origin.[32] After the ferment of the revolutionary period, polite American society—the group sending their children to college—looked to letters for stability and security. Colleges had become once again the conservative centers they had been in England. Literature was to support the existing social and economic arrangement, as well as to provide a stay for religion and morality. In keeping with the dominant national mood, poetry, drama, and fiction were expected to be optimistic about the future. Finally, given the concern for conserving

social order, artists were expected to look outward into society—
celebrating it, not pointing to its flaws. On all counts, Blair was just
what was wanted.

One other significant reason for Blair's popularity ought to be
mentioned. Blair emphasized written rather than oral discourse. As
the nineteenth century progressed, college rhetorics increasingly
came to focus on written language.[33] This was partly due to the beginnings of the specialization of college faculties, with elocution
teachers assuming more of the burden of instruction in oratory. It
was as much due to a more significant development. America was
changing from an oral culture to a print culture. Decision making in
business and government was more and more to rely on the imper-
sonal printed word, rather than face-to-face contact. The ability to
write effectively was becoming more important than the ability to
speak at public gatherings. The rhetoric needed was a rhetoric of
the printed word, and Blair provided for the need in America as he
had done in his own country.[34]

4

American Imitators

THE INFLUENCE OF BLAIR, CAMPBELL, AND WHATELY DOMI-
nated the field until after the Civil War. So persistent was their
influence that the American rhetorics that appeared during this
time were little more than restatements of the blessed trinity. The
Americans who ventured into the field—primarily clergymen, since
American colleges were run by clergymen—were operating within
a pervasive paradigm. As Kitzhaber points out, there was some dis-
agreement among them about whether rhetoric is an art or a science.[1] A closer look reveals, however, that this was an intramural
squabble fought within the arena circumscribed by eighteenth-
century rhetoric. One group emphasized Campbell, presenting
rhetoric as a scientific body of principles, grounded in human nature. The other saw rhetoric as an art, deriving its impulse from
Blair's belletristic position. These were tendencies only, however,
not substantive differences, since both camps were grounded in
Common Sense Realism. In this chapter I would like to consider
one writer from each group, Samuel P. Newman representing the
belletristic emphasis and Henry Day the psychological and scientific.

One clear statement of belletristic rhetoric is Newman's *A Practical System of Rhetoric*, published in 1827. Others that are written
in the same vein are George P. Quackenbos, *Advanced Course
of Composition and Rhetoric* (1855), James R. Boyd, *Elements of
Rhetoric and Literary Composition* (1844), Richard G. Parker, *Aids
to English Composition* (1845), and John S. Hart, *A Manual of Composition and Rhetoric* (1870). These tend to emphasize rhetoric as

written, rather than oral discourse, and are concerned with providing the principles of taste that will enable the student to write effectively.

The full title of Newman's textbook on writing—first published in 1827 and in its twentieth printing by 1846—gives a sense of its belletristic intent: *A Practical System of Rhetoric, or the Principles and Rules of Style, Inferred from Examples of Writing; to which is added a Historical Dissertation on English Style.* (He obviously felt that one ought to be able to tell a book from its cover.) His conception of rhetoric's role is offered at the start, under the heading of the advantages of studying rhetoric:

1. Some acquaintance with the philosophy of rhetoric.
2. The cultivation of the taste, and in connexion, the exercise of the imagination.
3. Skill in the use of language.
4. Skill in literary criticism.
5. The formation of a good style.[2]

The first item is dismissed, Newman explaining that the teacher should provide students with the necessary language of the faculties and direct them to an examination of their own minds. This matter is simply too abstract for a "practical" textbook. As for cultivating the taste, when Newman speaks of the "exercise of the imagination," his meaning is literal, the imagination being conceived as a muscle that needs a workout in order to function well. Skill in language use, the third item, involves the imitation of Campbell and Blair on usage, particularly Campbell, who is called the "Quintilian of English Literature." The fourth and fifth items, skill in literary criticism and style, are taken directly from Blair. Newman sees the two as interchangeable, the study of literature being the study of the effects of style. This study will in turn lead to effective reading and writing: "What is most necessary on the part of the instructor is, to direct the attention to specimens of different styles, and in some few instances to point out characteristic traits. The student, with this aid, will soon acquire sufficient knowledge and skill to apply the remarks found in the text-book himself."[3] These principles of style will be used in the student's own writing, Newman recommending that students attempt outlines and learn to construct sentences through translation. Finally, the teacher is directed to correct the student's composition and to offer encouragement.

The first chapter is entitled "On Thought as the Foundation of Good Writing." After promising to use the inductive method in discussing rhetorical principles, Newman announces that the chapter is to cover the content of discourse, that which appeals to the understanding, while the rest of the textbook will be concerned with the appeals to the imagination. Although this would seem to promise material on invention, in fact it means little more than general advice on being a careful observer. Thus, the student is told that he must have extensive knowledge, that he must have a disciplined mind, and that he must learn patient reflection. This is reduced to students cultivating the habit of looking closely at "the phenomena, both in the natural world and in the scenes of life," and following "their own thoughts . . . [to] trace out their connexions and relations."[4] Once again, however, no advice in generating material aside from the injunction to observe closely and record carefully is given: the material of discourse is self-evident when correct observation is undertaken. And so the rest of the chapter is given over to managerial advice. The student is told that he must arrange his ideas methodically and amplify them adequately. The different kinds of composition are briefly discussed, the forms of discourse chosen following Campbell: persuasive, argumentative, descriptive, and narrative. Newman finally offers information on the selection of a subject and structure of the essay—apparently from Whately—with advice on introductions, the essay body, and its divisions.

The rest of the textbook, matter dealing with the appeal to the imagination and emotion, is predictably reliant on Blair, with an occasional nod to Campbell. Chapter 2, "On Taste," takes up the distinction between the beautiful and the sublime, relying primarily on Blair, but adding material that is neither original nor striking. Newman then discusses the faculties involved in taste. He also claims to disagree with Blair on the definition of taste, but he is really just introducing a cavil. He closes this chapter with a section from Campbell on the fine and useful arts, neglecting to include Campbell's emphasis on oratorical persuasion as the highest art because of its inclusion of both. Newman's belletristic stance inevitably leads to the preference of the written over the oral.

Chapter 3 deals with the nature and objects of literary taste. Literature is extended to include, after Blair, poetry and fiction, as well as historical, epistolary, and essay writing. Newman relies on a distinction between literature and science, only to say he will include science in literature. His main interest in this chapter, however, is the examination of ornaments of style, explaining, "though not essential to the communication of the writer's thoughts, they are often highly useful."[5] The ornaments to be considered are simile, metaphor, allusion, and personification. In each case, Newman traces the appeal to taste, discovering its source in our nature, in "a fitness, or association, or some primary law of our nature."[6] The discussion is based on a mechanistic conception of figures and is technical and tedious in the extreme, leading us to pity the poor students who were asked to memorize it.

Chapter 5, on usage, and chapter 6, on style, are again from Campbell and Blair. Language is regarded as a mechanical sign system, separate from thought, throughout. The qualities of good style—correctness, perspicuity, vivacity, euphony—are adapted from Campbell. The kinds of style—e.g., concise and diffuse, forcible and vehement—are lifted directly from Blair. Newman next offers a section on each of the different kinds of literature listed earlier, although he excludes poetry, presumably having given enough space to this matter already. He also offers only two pages on oratory, again showing his emphasis on writing. The instructional part of the text closes with a set of exercises, consisting of short passages that display various kinds of literature and an analysis of each using the appropriate stylistic principles. The last 45 pages are given over to the "Historical Dissertation on English Style," again applying the abstract principles discussed earlier to writers from Mandeville to Dryden. It is without distinction.

Henry Day's *Elements of the Art of Rhetoric* is the clearest example of Campbell's philosophic rhetoric in this period. Others are M. B. Hope, *The Princeton Text-Book in Rhetoric* (1859) and John Bascom, *Philosophy of Rhetoric* (1866). All emphasize rhetoric as oratory and attempt to ground the discipline in a science of human nature based on Common Sense Realism.

Henry Day's *Elements of the Art of Rhetoric* was published in 1850 and the similar *Art of Discourse* in 1867. Day considered himself an innovator in rhetorical theory, correcting the ancients as well as such contemporaries as Whately. In fact, he was in every way thoroughly the student of Campbell, carrying out the Scottish rhetorician's plan in detail. Day's genuine contribution to rhetorical theory, in fact, is that he saw the full implications of Campbell's scheme.

Day regards rhetoric as the science of adapting oral discourse to an audience, a clear echo of Campbell. He felt that his important service to rhetoric was restoring invention to its proper place, and his definition of invention promises to do so: "the art of supplying the requisite thought in kind and form for discourse."[7] He goes on to explain, however, that invention includes both providing the thought and the arrangement of discourse. This seems eccentric until we realize that Day is the first American rhetorician to apply the managerial notion of invention found in Campbell and Whately. By invention, Day means discovering the faculty in the hearer that the speaker wishes to affect, and then shaping the message so that it achieves its end. In other words, invention is not discovering what to say, but managing what we have discovered outside the rhetorical process so that it produces a desired outcome in the mind of the hearer.

Day thus devised an approach that John Franklin Genung will later simplify and use with great consequences for the twentieth century. He explains that since the "possible immediate objects of all proper discourse are but four in number, vis.: EXPLANATION, CONVICTION, EXCITATION, and PERSUASION,"[8] he will take up each in turn, discussing the principles of invention appropriate to each. These four are an early version of the forms of discourse, each designed to act on the appropriate faculty: explanation appealing to the understanding, conviction to reason, excitation to the feelings, and persuasion to the will. Persuasion, as in Campbell, moreover, is the highest expression of oratory because it involves all the faculties. What Day calls invention is actually arrangement, shaping the discourse so as to appeal to the appropriate faculty. Unity is important because no more than one faculty ought to dominate in the appeal made by an address: "The work of invention can never proceed with ease or success unless unity is strictly observed—unless the single subject and the single object of the discourse be clearly apprehended, and that object be steadily and undeviatingly pursued."[9] Day's advice is to keep one's eye on the subject considered, and to present it to the reader by shaping it to appeal to the appropriate faculty, being careful not to confuse the issue by appealing to too many faculties at once. Since faculties function discretely and sequentially, more than one object at a time will cause confusion. Day goes on to devote half the book to ways of developing each of the four forms of discourse. I should also mention that he includes narration and description under explanation, as well as analysis, exemplification, and comparison and contrast—in the last introducing something of the Aristotelian commonplaces into his scheme, a device that will become popular much later.

The second part of the textbook deals with style, calling this time on Blair as well as Campbell. Day in each case acknowledges his source. It is like the first part in following a rigidly organized pattern, scrupulously dividing each item considered into its parts and considering each part in detail. (The rigorous analysis is reminiscent of Ramistic schemes.) This method, of course, aided students in their attempts to memorize the material. As Kitzhaber explains, furthermore, Day's textbook, especially its treatment of invention, "was a striking example of the abstract and theoretical approach to rhetorical doctrine that was typical of the fifties and sixties."[10] Day is important in the history of American rhetoric because he realized the full implications of Campbell's managerial scheme of invention and presented them in a form that was simplified and embraced later on. As we shall see, this simplification involved other distortions of Campbell and Day that were unfortunate.

These two rhetorics—one belletristic and the other psychological and scientific—were typical of those studied at American colleges after the Civil War. During this time, there had been attempts to change American colleges, to bring them more in line with the sympathies of a democratic society on the one hand, and to make them centers of learning on the other. But these attempts had failed as colleges became the centers of conservatism, looked upon as providing training in character through religion and the intellectual discipline of a narrowly defined literary education. The most important statement of the purposes of the American college from 1825 to at least 1870 was the Yale Report of 1828. It argued for the mechanical faculty psychology of Common Sense Realism: "The two great points to be gained in intellectual culture, are the *discipline* and the *furniture* of the mind; expanding its powers, and storing it with knowledge."[11] The ancient subjects did this the best: mathematics, classical languages and literature, and "moral and intellectual phi-

losophy"—the last drawn primarily from the doctrine of the particular religious group that controlled the college. As Rudolph explains, "Even the use of textbooks and recitations was defended as
being superior to an arrangement that would send students into li-
braries, there to read the sources and conflicting authorities."[12] The
college was to train aristocrats, a class of men whose education was
intentionally made to be unrelated to the affairs of the larger society, resting instead on eternal principles. The days of this system,
however, were soon to be ended.

5

Emerson and Romantic Rhetoric

ANY CONSIDERATION OF ROMANTIC RHETORIC TODAY NECESSARILY encounters difficulties. It is a commonplace of contemporary discussions of rhetoric to regard the romantic frame of mind as staunchly anti-rhetorical.[1] Rhetoric is a social construction—this thinking goes—providing a scheme of thought intent on communicating shared meaning among individuals and groups. The romantics, with their insistence on the private and personal in discovering and communicating truth, deny the inherently communal nature of the art, thereby abolishing rhetoric's reason for being. Ralph Waldo Emerson, however, offers the best argument against this line of thought. In this chapter I would like to demonstrate Emerson's effort to create a romantic rhetoric that, despite its emphasis on the individual, is social and democratic, combining the comprehensiveness of Aristotelian rhetoric with a post-Kantian epistemology. At the same time, it is a system designed to be counteractive to the eighteenth-century rhetoric of its day.

Emerson was, of course, a skillful practitioner of oratory, and most of his essays were first presented as lectures. He was also, however, a serious student of rhetorical theory; on more than one occasion he regretted that no college had seen fit to offer him a professorship of rhetoric.[2] Furthermore, as Sheldon W. Liebman has demonstrated, Emerson's initial loyalty to Hugh Blair's *Lectures on Rhetoric and Belles Lettres* was followed by a conscious rejection of the Scottish rhetorician and the formation of an alternative original in theory and practice.[3] Still, there are undeniable difficulties in discussing Emerson's rhetoric. None of these, however, need to be insuperable. Emerson in no one place sets forth a systematic statement of his rhetorical theory. But this can be said of almost any feature of his thought, and in "Nature" (1836) and in the two essays entitled "Eloquence" (1847 and 1867), Emerson does offer a compact and accessible account of his position. Emerson also emphasizes oratory over written expression and tends to equate the best products of both with poetry. This, however, was a characteristic of the transcendentalist approach to discourse. As F. O. Matthiessen explains, "In declaring that the best prose becomes poetic, that the sublimest speech is a poem, Emerson was voicing the special desire of the transcendentalists to break through all restricting divisions. But in his tendency to link poets and orators whenever he listed the various acts, he was responding to a more common and widespread belief of his time. . . . To a degree that we have lost sight of, oratory was then the basis for other forms of writing, and its modes of expression left a mark on theirs."[4] Thus, in emphasizing oratory in his discussion of rhetoric, Emerson is including written discourse, even when he does not explicitly say so (although he often does). We should also be prepared to discover that what Emerson says of the rhetor is often identical to what he elsewhere claims for the poet.

Several excellent treatments of Emerson's rhetorical thought are available in the literature. These tend to fall into two categories. The first sees Emerson as a romantic individualist, concerned primarily with rhetoric as the expression of the self, without regard for political or social concerns. The second emphasizes Emerson's commitment to democracy—his positioning of the rhetor at the center of political and social action.[5] This position seems to me the more accurate description of Emerson's thought. I will argue that Emerson's rhetoric is preeminently concerned with the role of discourse in the public domain, centering on the place of communication in a modern democracy. Before doing so, I would like to consider the alternative reading.

Those who see Emerson as advocating a rhetoric of self-expression place him—either consciously or unconsciously—within the Platonic tradition that denies the possibility of a rhetoric of public discourse.[6] (There is another tradition attributed to Plato that I will consider later.) For Plato, truth is not based on sensory experience. It is discovered through an internal apprehension, a private vision of a realm that transcends the material. As Robert Cushman explains in *Therapeia*, "The central theme of Platonism regarding knowledge is that truth is not brought to man, but man to truth."[7] This means that knowledge must be discovered by the individual: it can be learned but not taught. Rhetoric, then, cannot communicate truth, but can only bring auditors to the point at which they are prepared to discover truth on their own, in their private, visionary pursuits. For Plato, the rhetorical experience encourages speaker and listener to break out of their ordinary perceptual set, to become free of the bondage to the material world and past error. Rhetoric is subversive, a disruption of ordinary experience, requiring new ways of perceiving in order to overcome long-held conventions and opinions. Plato's epistemology further leads to a unique view of language. Since truth is found in the supersensory, in a realm beyond the physical world, ordinary language cannot express it; words, after all, refer to the sensory realm, the world of flux. At times, Plato insists that language can never express ultimate truth, but can only lead to the correction of error, preparing auditors to see correctly in a private, incommunicable perception. In the *Republic* and in the *Phaedrus*, however, he suggests that through the use of metaphor, language can approach the expression of the infinite ideal. In the latter, he thus admits the possibility that a speaker who knows the truth and relies on metaphor—as he himself does—can suggest ultimate truth, not simply correct error.

Roberta K. Ray makes the most compelling case for placing Emerson within this framework, although she does not explicitly call upon Plato. Emerson, she explains, is a philosophical idealist who sees the basis of reality in a spiritual realm that underlies all material existence. This realm is variously referred to as God or the Over-Soul and embodies the ideals of truth, goodness, and beauty. Nature, the material world, is the opposite of the ideal, but corresponds to it. Ray explains: "The material world is not of value in and of itself. It is only important to man insofar as it can bring him insight into the spiritual world." The main use of Nature is to provide individuals with the materials for metaphor: the exploitation of "the outer world to explain the inner world of mind and spirit."[8] The purpose of human existence is to discover God, the repository of ideas, and this is achieved through the use of Reason, the intuitive, visionary faculty that provides access to the infinite. Understanding is a lower faculty that is entrusted, according to Ray, with "the enthymeme and inductive reasoning to determine probable truth in the everyday affairs of men, in the courtrooms and political assemblies." This area of attention, the traditional realm of rhetoric, is, however, outside of Emerson's concern as philosopher and rhetorician. Rhetoric is to focus on our attempts to find God, not to live in the material world, so that "Emerson's orator must rely primarily on his intuition to provide the higher truths which men seek."[9]

Ray likewise places Emerson within the Platonic tradition (again, by implication) in making ideal truth the product of inspiration, a gift bestowed on a passive recipient who is using reason correctly. This truth cannot be communicated. All that the orator can do is to prepare auditors to discover it on their own. She explains: "According to Emerson's philosophy, one man cannot communicate truth to another, since truth is a state of mind. . . . The communicator can serve as a midwife helping others to give birth to their own thoughts."[10] The orator achieves this through disrupting the everyday perceptions of the audience: "The true preacher or teacher does not instruct. He agitates. He provokes." By challenging our erroneous versions of truth, the rhetor can lead individuals to look within in order "to see, feel, and live by that truth which comes from the Over-Soul, that lies within them waiting to be animated."[11]

Ray's reading of Emerson is compelling, all the more because it represents a version shared by others. In fact, as I have argued elsewhere, it articulates a rhetorical vein in America that is today being mined in the composition textbooks of such figures as Ken Macrorie, William Coles, Jr., Donald Stewart, and James E. Miller and Stephen Judy.[12] Ray has read widely and carefully, and she scrupulously documents her case in Emerson's work. Additional evidence for her position is also provided by Liebman, who finds in Emerson's journals a description of automatic writing, composing under the influence of inspiration without the interference of conscious thought. (Liebman hastens to point out, however, that this practice did not keep Emerson from laborious revision.)[13] Ray can make her case, however, only by repeatedly denying that Emerson was concerned with social and political matters. Yet the most casual reading of Emerson's essays demonstrates that this is simply not the case. Ray focuses on essays in which Emerson is most concerned with philosophical theory, simultaneously ignoring those in which he deals with the practical affairs of society. Most notably, she makes only slight reference to Emerson's two essays on eloquence, the very works in which he wishes to show the value of rhetoric in a democracy. Ray's error of omission leads to a distorted reading of Emerson's thought on rhetoric. This distortion is exacerbated by her insistence that Emerson embraced a Platonic epistemology, an interpretation that—as I plan to demonstrate—will not hold up.

The best statement on Emerson as a rhetorician of public discourse—the creator of a scheme for a modern democracy—is William S. Tacey's "Emerson on Eloquence." His argument rests almost exclusively on the two "Eloquence" essays, ignoring their philosophical base in Emerson's thought. In its own way, it is as incomplete as is Ray's reading, although not as limited in its interpretation. Since I will be covering all the ground of this essay, there is no need to rehearse it here. In the following, I would like to show how Emerson fuses a post-Kantian philosophical idealism with democratic social theory, placing rhetoric at the heart of the democratic experience.

Despite his admiration for Plato, Emerson's philosophical idealism is not Platonic. His position is indeed closer to such moderns as Ernst Cassirer and Susanne Langer. Emerson starts with the difficult question of the relation between subject and object. Common Sense Realism takes the object, the material realm, as the ground of the real. Aristotle finds the real in the rational, while Plato looks to the supersensory, the absolute, for ultimate reality. Emerson departs from all as he locates the real in the fusion of the sensual and ideal. Reality is a human construction, joining the world of ideas to the material object in an act of creative perception. The sensory realm by itself is lifeless matter. The ideal by itself is meaningless abstraction. Knowledge is possible only in the interaction of the two.

This is not to deny that for Emerson the ground of reality is the ideal. He will not, however, contend that the material is illusory, mere flux and phantom. To do so, Emerson explains in "Nature," is to exist "in the splendid labyrinth of my perceptions . . . denying substantive being to men and women."[14] The external world actually exists and is a part of the divine scheme. The ideal is, of course, identified with God, the intelligence informing the universe, but it exerts its force only through individuals: "Therefore, that spirit, that is, the Supreme Being, does not build up nature around us, but puts it forth through us, as the life of the tree puts forth new branches and leaves through the pores of the old."[15] The ideal then becomes that which the individual brings to the material world. It is the store of ideas that shape and make sense of human experience, and these ideas have no meaning apart from this concrete experience. The external world, moreover, suggests ideas to the individual: "Nature is made to conspire with spirit to emancipate us. Certain mechanical changes, a small alteration in our local position, apprizes us of dualism."[16] At the most elementary level, for example, nature leads to the discovery of physical laws, themselves ideas that arise in our experience of nature. Thus, for Emerson, the ideal can be known only through its manifestation in the external world. At the same time, the external world can lead to ideas. The inner and outer have no meaning apart from each other. Truth is a product of a relationship; its source is neither subject nor object, but is located at the point of intersection of the two. Emerson can be seen as anticipating modern epistemology, arguing for reality as the product of the interaction of the perceiver and that which is perceived.

The key to Emerson's epistemology is located in language. Emerson makes the individual the center of the universe, creating meaning through the fusion of idea and matter, of subject and object. The medium of this fusion is language. Because it unites sensory objects with ideas, language is inherently metaphoric, combining the conceptual tenor with its material vehicle. Emerson takes Plato's special use of metaphor and makes it the paradigm of all language behavior.

This is elucidated in Emerson's chapter on language in "Nature." He begins with three postulates:

1. Words are signs of natural facts.
2. Particular natural facts are symbols of particular spiritual facts.
3. Nature is the symbol of spirit.[17]

Emerson's explanation of these begins in a Platonic vein. Words are the signs of concrete objects, the material world thus constituting the basis of language. Individuals are also aware of a realm beyond the mere sensory—the world of ideas—providing access to such concepts as "Justice, Truth, Love, Freedom."[18] The individual can use only natural language, the signs of the material world, to express this realm. Because of its sensory base, however, this language must be used metaphorically, relying on words referring to the sensory to suggest what transcends the sensory. Emerson departs from the Platonic scheme, however, in making metaphoric language the norm, rather than the exceptional province of the philosopher. For Plato, attention to the finite world misleads us in our search for the truth. For Emerson, the perception of material nature encourages the perception of the ideal. Nature in its normal operation suggests the ideal as it simultaneously provides the language in which the ideal can be expressed. Without the language of the sensory, the ideal cannot be made manifest. Conversely, without the ideal, the world of nature is mere sense data without order or meaning. The point of intersection between outside and inside is language.

Emerson is explicit in enunciating this view. "Every appearance in nature," he explains, "corresponds to some state of the mind, and that state of the mind can only be described by presenting that natural appearance as its picture."[19] Ideal and real are dependent upon each other, and the agency of their manifestation is metaphoric language. All individuals in the normal course of experience engage in this use of metaphor:

> The moment our discourse rises above the ground line of familiar facts and is inflamed with passion or exalted by thought, it clothes itself in images. A man conversing in earnest, if he watch his intellectual processes, will find that a material image more or less luminous arises in his mind, contemporaneous with every thought, which furnishes the vestment of the thought. Hence, good writing and brilliant discourse are perpetual allegories. The imagery is spontaneous. It is the blending of experience with the present action of the mind. It is proper creation.[20]

This use of metaphor is the paradigm for all language use: "These are not the dreams of a few poets, here and there, but man is an analogist, and studies relations in all objects. He is placed in the center of beings and a ray of relation passes from every other being to him. And neither can man be understood without these objects, nor these objects without man."[21] The individual unites the material and ideal in metaphor. Subject and object have meaning only in the creation of the unifying symbol.

Emerson's post-Kantian epistemology is at the base of his rhetorical system. It is true that in "Nature" Emerson speaks disparagingly of the uses of language in the realm of public affairs. This comes in the section in which he elucidates his third postulate of language: "Nature is the symbol of spirit." After explaining that metaphor constitutes the core of all language—indeed, that it constitutes reality itself in fusing ideas and objects—Emerson notes the wastefulness of using metaphor for "pepper-corn information" and "the dictionary and grammar of . . . municipal speech."[22] The highest aim of language is philosophical, the explanation of the fundamental conditions of the universe. This statement, however, should not be allowed to negate his genuine concern for the role of rhetoric in "municipal speech," displayed both in the first two parts of this section on language and in other essays. It would even be possible to argue that the two "Eloquence" essays represent a rethinking of his earlier position, appearing, as they do, considerably later than "Nature" (1836)—the first in 1847 and the second in 1867. As I will show, however, there is no need to do so; the two essays are not irreconcilable.

Earlier, I discussed the tradition that places Plato among those who deny the possibility of a rhetoric of public discourse, seeing the rhetor as an individual who is loyal to private vision without regard for the larger community. Richard M. Weaver has argued for another conception of Plato's stance on rhetoric. Despite the harsh criticism Plato levels at rhetoric, Weaver explains, he offers the possibility of a rhetoric of public affairs in the *Phaedrus*. Weaver sums up this revised position: "We now see the true rhetorician as a noble lover of good, who works through dialectic and through poetic or analogic association. However he is compelled to modulate by the peculiar features of an occasion, this is his method."[23] These elements are the distinguishing features of Emerson's rhetoric as well —the rhetor as lover of truth, dialectician, and analogist who is responsive to his auditors. The important difference is that Emerson erects his system on a post-Kantian epistemology and a democratic egalitarianism.

In his "Eloquence" essays, Emerson is concerned with rhetoric in the practical affairs of a democracy. Here he has in mind "the bar, the senate, journalism, and the pulpit,"[24] as well as town hall gatherings, asserting that rhetoric "is eminently that art which only flourishes in free countries."[25] In such societies, "every man is an orator."[26] Emerson repeatedly asserts that the gift of eloquence is universal, or is at least, "only the exaggeration of a talent that is universal."[27] Eloquence is a necessary consequence of the ability to create meaning through language. The individual in a democratic state is, moreover, morally obligated to take part in public affairs; it is a condition of citizenship. Emerson calls upon Plato in support of his position: "Plato says that the punishment which the wise suffer who refuse to take part in the government, is, to live under the government of worse men; and the like regret is suggested to all the auditors, as the penalty of abstaining to speak,—that they shall hear worse orators than themselves."[28] Public discourse is a necessary element in the democratic process: "The eloquence of one stimulates all the rest, some up to the speaking-point, and all others to a degree that makes them good receivers and conductors, and they avenge themselves for their enforced silence by increased loquacity on their return to the fireside."[29] We recall the importance of language in Emerson's thought: discussion is necessary in order that idea and experience may be united in the creation of meaning. The democratic ideal of free discussion is implicated in Emerson's very epistemology.

Emerson's definition of his democratic rhetoric locates its distinguishing feature in the persuasive presentation of truth. He had already suggested this in "Nature," where he states, "A man's power to connect his thought with its proper symbol, and so to utter it, depends on the simplicity of his character, that is, upon his love of truth and his desire to communicate it without loss."[30] In the essays on eloquence, he expands this notion. In the first, he ascribes to Plato the definition of rhetoric as "the art of ruling the minds of men," adding, "yet the end of eloquence is—is it not?—to alter in a pair of hours, perhaps in a half hour's discourse, the convictions and habits of years."[31] In the second, his emphasis is on the audience: "Eloquence is *the power to translate a truth into language perfectly intelligible to the person to whom you speak*."[32] (Italics in original) Rhetoric must be committed to truth, it must be persuasive, and it must consider the particular audience.

Emerson's insistence that the rhetor is to know the truth and be able to translate it into language intelligible to the particular audience is a direct extension of his epistemology. The speaker must be sure "that he keeps his feet ever on a fact,"[33] but that he brings to facts a set of ideas that give them order and meaning:

The orator possesses no information which his hearers have not, yet he teaches them to see the thing with his eyes. By the new placing, the circumstances acquire new solidity and worth. Every fact gains consequently by his naming it, and trifles become important. His expressions fix themselves in men's memories, and fly from mouth to mouth. His mind has some new principle of order.[34]

The rhetor offers the wholeness of the dialectical product of idea and experience. The message is a reproduction of "the order of Nature itself,"[35] by which Emerson means that the best discourse offers the wholeness of perception that results when perceiver and perceived, idea and sense, are unified in the highest vision: "I esteem this to be its [rhetoric's] perfection,—when the orator sees through all masks to the eternal scale of truth, in such sort that he can hold up before the eyes of men the fact of today steadily to that standard, thereby making the great great, and small small, which is the true way to astonish and reform mankind."[36] Fact and thought must be united for truth to prevail: "If you would correct my false view of facts,—hold up to me the same facts in the true order of thought, and I cannot go back from the new conviction."[37]

As we have seen in "Nature," language is crucial in creating meaning, and Emerson spells out its role in public discourse. Language must be metaphoric:

The orator must be, to a certain extent, a poet. We are such imaginative creatures that nothing so works on the human mind, barbarous or civil, as a trope. Condense some daily experience into a glowing symbol, and an audience is electrified. They feel as if they already possessed some new sight and power over a fact which they can detach, and so completely master in thought. . . . Put the argument into a concrete shape, into an image,—some hard phrase, sound and solid as a ball, which they can see and handle and carry home with them,—and the course is half won.[38]

Metaphor unites idea and matter, embodying truth in the only way possible. Only through its use can the speaker persuade the reluctant auditor—find "a statement possible of that truth which he is most unwilling to receive."[39] In keeping with his democratic impulse, Emerson insists that this language not be confined to that of polite society: "The orator must command the whole scale of the language, from the most elegant to the most low and vile. Every one has felt how superior in force is the language of the street to that of the academy. The street must be one of his schools."[40] This does not mean that discourse should be rude or contrary to correct usage; it is to be "plain speech, chastened, however, by the schools into correctness."[41] But language must be grounded in concrete experience, "grounded on the plainest narrative."[42] Only through the interaction of the concrete experience and the idea in a metaphoric display can meaning be established, and established persuasively. As Emerson asserts, "if the pupil be of a texture to bear it, the best university that can be recommended to a man of ideas is the gauntlet of the mobs."[43]

Contact with all of a language's resources is important for another reason. After a time, metaphors lose their capacity to body forth truth, degenerating to the status of lifeless objects or self-serving abstractions. The metaphor is no longer the union of object and idea, but becomes a meaningless cliché or is used to serve private, sectarian interests. In "Nature," Emerson explains this process:

> The corruption of man is followed by the corruption of language. When simplicity of character and the sovereignty of ideas is broken up by the prevalence of secondary desires,—the desire of riches, of pleasure, of power, and of praise,—the duplicity and falsehood take place of simplicity and truth, the power over nature as an interpreter of the will is in a degree lost; new imagery ceases to be created, and old words are perverted to stand for things which are not; a paper currency is employed, when there is no bullion in the vaults. In due time the fraud is manifest, and words lose all power to stimulate the understanding or the affections. Hundreds of writers may be found in every long-civilized nation who for a short time believe and make others believe that they see and utter truths, who do not of themselves clothe one thought in its natural garment, but who feed unconsciously on the language created by the primary writers of the country, those, namely, who hold primarily on nature.[44]

When this happens, new metaphors must be created, once again embodying truth in a fresh union of object and idea: "But wise men pierce this rotten diction and fasten words again to visible things; so that picturesque language is at once a commanding certificate that he who employs it is a man in alliance with truth and God."[45] Truth remains always and everywhere the same, but new metaphors must be continually generated in order to express it. Thus, to limit the language which an individual uses is to limit the capacity to see and utter truth. As in Wittgenstein, the limits of one's language are the limits of one's world.

I mentioned earlier Emerson's contention that all individuals are orators, all have the capacity for rhetorical expression. But the desire and willingness of a person to speak are not enough. What is required is inspiration, but not the inspiration that emanates from the absolute. Instead, the impulse to speak comes from the occasions that continually arise in a democracy. Once again, truth and the language to express it are as much the result of what an individual brings to an experience as what the experience brings to the individual: "For the triumph of art somewhat more must still be required, namely a reinforcing of man from events, so as to give the double force of reason and destiny. In transcendent eloquence, there was ever some crisis in affairs, such as could deeply engage the man to the cause he pleads, and draw all the wide powers to a point."[46] Emerson is here speaking of what today is called the rhetorical exigency, a compelling reason to speak or write. This compulsion, moreover, itself arises out of the dialectical conflict of opposing alternatives that are the norm in a democracy: "But the conditions for eloquence always exist. It is always dying out of famous places and appearing in corners. Wherever the polarities meet, wherever the fresh moral sentiment, the instinct of freedom and duty, come in direct opposition to fossil conservatism and the thirst of gain, the spark will pass."[47] Rhetoric once again is the product of the individual committed to truth and the appropriate occasion, both of which are encouraged in a democratic community.

Emerson's rhetoric is everywhere dialectical—the result of the confrontation of idea and object, of speaker and event, of political opinion and political opinion. This same principle holds sway in Emerson's treatment of the rhetor and the audience. In a journal entry, Emerson notes, "Propose no methods, prepare no words, select no traditions, but fix your eyes on the audience, and the fit word will utter itself."[48] The importance of the audience in deter-

mining the rhetorical product is emphasized everywhere in Emerson. This does not mean "addressing the prejudices of the com-
pany."[49] Instead, the rhetor is to engage in a dialectic with the
audience, allowing its unique characteristics to stimulate him to discover his message:

> An audience is not a simple addition of the individuals that compose it.
> Their sympathy gives them a certain social organism, which fills each
> member, in his own degree, and most of all the orator, as a jar in a battery
> is charged with the whole electricity of the battery. No one can survey
> the face of an excited assembly, without being apprised of new oppor-
> tunity for painting in fire human thought, and being agitated to agitate.[50]

As John H. Sloan has demonstrated, Emerson's notion of his relation to the audience is a direct contradiction of eighteenth-century
notions of the speaker adapting to the listener.[51] Emerson instead
argues that the audience must be made to adapt to the speaker.
By this he means appealing to the audience so that it enters the
speaker's world, perceiving the world through the speaker's language. Emerson explains:

> Of course the interest of the audience and of the orator conspire. It is
> well with them only when his influence is complete; then only they are
> well pleased. Especially he consults his power by making instead of tak-
> ing his theme. If he should attempt to instruct the people in that which
> they already know, he would fail; by making them wise in that which he
> knows, he has the advantage of the assembly every moment.[52]

The orator must carry his audience with him, instead of being directed by it. This, again, involves the use of the appropriate metaphoric language: "The power of the speech is, that it is perfectly understood by all, and I believe it to be true that when any orator at
the bar or in the Senate rises in his thought, he descends in his language,—that is, when he rises to any height of thought or of passion
he comes down to a language level with the ear of all his audience."[53] And Emerson throughout maintains his respect for the audience: "There is also something excellent in every audience,—the
capacity of virtue."[54]

Finally, Emerson makes his rhetoric central to democratic society because of his conviction that language is action. This is perhaps the single most powerful argument against regarding his rhetoric as divorced from the concerns of public life. Emerson's journal for 1835 begins with the motto, "To think is to act." Because material reality is always involved in thought, because the idea without an object is literally inconceivable, ideas always have consequences for human behavior. Language is thought and thing combined, so that language is always action. This necessarily means that the rhetor is essential in the activities of public life: "His speech is not to be distinguished from action. It is the electricity of action. It is action, as the general's word of command or chart of battle is action. I must feel that the speaker compromises himself to his auditory, comes for something,—it is a cry on the perilous edge of the fight,—or let him be silent."[55] In another place, he says of the orator, "Let him see that his speech is not differentiated from action; that when he has spoken he has not done nothing, nor done wrong, but has cleared his own skirts, has engaged himself to wholesome exertion."[56] And it is this insistence on the relation of language to action that makes rhetoric indispensable to a democratic society:

> If there ever was a country where eloquence was a power, it is the United States. Here is room for every degree of it, on every one of its ascending stages,—that of useful speech, in our commercial, manufacturing, railroad and educational conventions; that of political advice and persuasion on the grandest theatre, reaching, as all good men trust, into a vast future, and so compelling the best thought and noblest administrative ability that the citizen can offer. And here are the service of science, the demands of art, and the lessons of religion to be brought home to the instant practice of thirty millions of people. Is it not worth the ambition of every generous youth to train and arm his mind with all the resources of knowledge, of method, of grace and of character, to serve such a constituency?[57]

I have tried to demonstrate that Emerson's rhetoric is first and foremost a system of thought designed to reconcile philosophical idealism with the demands of a democratic society. I am convinced that those who find in Emerson a rhetoric of self-expression are mistaken, even though this reading may be used in support of modern expressionist rhetoric. Emerson was a diverse and fecund thinker whose influence in rhetoric, as in poetic, has taken remarkable turns. Emerson never received his professorship in rhetoric, so it is impossible to know how he would have taught the composing process. Judging from the perspective I have offered here and from his own practice, it most certainly would have emphasized journal keeping, the role of the rhetorical context in invention, and extensive revision. I suspect that the composition textbooks of Fred Newton Scott, Joseph Villiers Denney, and Gertrude Buck appearing later in the century—to be discussed shortly—represent a close approximation of the kind of classroom techniques Emerson would have followed. I should add that there is no evidence that they were consciously following Emerson's lead. As Donald Stewart pointed out to me, however, in John Dewey, Emerson's staunch admirer, there is a possible point of contact, since Dewey and Scott were congenial colleagues at the University of Michigan for a time.

The reasons that Emerson's democratic rhetoric had such little effect on the college curriculum during most of the century probably have to do with the nature of higher education itself. Until after the Civil War, colleges were conservative institutions, run by Protestant clergymen who subscribed to the philosophy of Common Sense Realism. In short, these schools were not democratic in spirit, despite the lip service they paid to democracy in order to survive. The rhetorics they taught were designed for the conservative lawyers, clergymen, or civic leaders their students were destined to become. The speaker they wished to train was looked upon as an authority speaking in behalf of the *status quo*. Truth was regarded as external to the rhetorical act, fixed and certain in the nature of things, discovered through the use of the faculties, but still accessible only to those who had learned to use the faculties correctly. The audience was involved in the rhetorical act only in that each member was composed of a set of discrete, abstractly described faculties that must be addressed. The language used was to be the language of the educated, meaning the often stultifying diction and syntax of the educated clergy and the classes they served. As Rudolph explains, "The choice . . . was between adopting a course of study that appealed to all classes or adhering to a course that appealed to one class." Most colleges selected the second alternative. As a result, by the 1850s college enrollment in New England was declining both in actual numbers and in proportion to the growth of the population as a whole.[58]

Emerson's rhetoric, not restricted to securing a desired effect on the audience, was attempting to restore the search for truth to the composing act. Truth, moreover, is organic, is a holistic product growing out of the entire rhetorical situation—reality, speaker, listener, and language. All are involved in discovery and each changes in response to each. These are not static entities to be considered through mechanical calculation. In its emphasis on truth, in its comprehensiveness, and in its social orientation, Emerson's rhetoric rivals Aristotelian rhetoric. Its noetic field, furthermore, places it at the center of the intellectual currents of the nineteenth century as well as those of today. As we have seen in I. A. Richards and Kenneth Burke, one does not have to be a philosophical idealist to see reality as the convergence of perceiver and perceived with language as the agent of mediation.

6

Current-Traditional Rhetoric

THE SUPREMACY OF EIGHTEENTH-CENTURY RHETORIC WAS FI-
nally challenged after the Civil War. As the nation changed, so did
the colleges and their sense of purpose. Composition classes were
dealing with different students and viewing them from a different
perspective. A rash of textbooks appeared between 1870 and the
end of the century, and, although these most often displayed the
use of ideas found in Blair, Campbell, and Whately, two distinctly
new versions of the composing process prevailed. One grew out
of the work of Fred Newton Scott, Joseph Villiers Denney, and
Gertrude Buck. This was the most revolutionary classroom rhetoric
to appear in the century, representing a new romanticism. Consideration of it will be reserved to the next chapter. The other new
rhetoric was finally embodied in the textbooks of three figures:
Adams Sherman Hill and Barrett Wendell, both of Harvard, and
John Franklin Genung of Amherst. In this chapter, I would like to
trace the development of this second conception of composing—a
view today labeled current-traditional rhetoric. Before doing so, I
would like to consider the changes in the American college that encouraged the new rhetorics.

After the Civil War the American college became transformed,
moving increasingly toward a commitment to serving all the citizens
of society—not just an aristocratic elite—and toward an encouragement of learning and free inquiry. The domination of colleges by
clergymen was beginning to weaken even before the war as governing boards came to be occupied by men of affairs. After the war,
these groups were instrumental in pushing for change in the curriculum, arguing for an education that prepared students for work in

this life, not for rewards in the next. The first schools to replace the classical course of studies, however, were not private ones, but state institutions, especially in the West, now provided with state funds to serve the agricultural and commercial interests of their growing populations. These schools often received funds that were previously allotted to private schools. Eventually, private institutions realized that if they were to continue to attract students, they, too, would have to introduce the new practical curriculum, although, it should be noted, a number—Johns Hopkins and Harvard, for example—were themselves leaders in reform.

In looking for ways that higher education could meet the demands of the growing economy, Americans turned to the German model. This meant a redefinition of purpose, a new curriculum, and a new way of defining the student. Rudolph succinctly describes the new college as it was shaped at Johns Hopkins:

> For the acceptance of revealed religious truth the new university in Baltimore substituted a search for scientific truth. For preparation for life in the next world it substituted a search for an understanding of this world. Johns Hopkins elevated man's reason to a position it had not before attained in the United States. It released the energies of scholarship, combined them with the national impulse to human betterment and material progress. The task it set for itself was immense and unending, and in time the spirit of Johns Hopkins would penetrate everywhere.[1]

The new American college was to allow the scientific and other new disciplines into the curriculum and provide, for the first time, an elective system. At some schools, especially state universities, this meant abandoning classical studies, complete with the cancellation of entrance requirements that insisted on an elementary knowledge of Greek and Latin. At most institutions, however, the new scientific courses were offered alongside the old classical offerings. The crucial difference was that an elective system enabled the student to choose the courses he wanted. Harvard under Charles William Eliot was the most extreme in its elective system, reducing required courses to freshmen in 1894, and decreasing even these to a year of freshman rhetoric in 1897.[2] Most colleges introduced a more modified system, asking students to fulfill area requirements from the courses of their choice. The required curriculum was, by the end of the century, hard to find, and the introduction of choice meant that many of the courses in the old curriculum died from inattention.

The new college was to serve the middle class, was to become an agent of upward social mobility. It was based on an educational psychology that abandoned mental discipline and the training of the faculties in favor of a view emphasizing individual differences and the importance of the student's pursuing his own natural talents. The new psychology was an obvious embodiment of the American faith in the possibilities of the individual when left to his own resources, unhindered by the prejudices of social class or institutional interference. The new college was nonetheless a middle-class college, committed to material success and progress in this world. Still, at its best, it was able to combine the Jeffersonian insistence on excellence with the Jacksonian demand for numbers.[3]

The new college profoundly affected the teaching of writing, bringing about a pedagogy shaped by the interests of the middle class. During the last quarter of the century, more and more students were attending college as the economy expanded and the need for skills provided by the new colleges grew. Most schools, both private and public, began to view themselves as serving the needs of business and industry. Citizens demanded it, students demanded it, and, most important, business leaders—the keepers of the funds—demanded it. The ability to write effectively—then as now—was one of the skills that all agreed was essential to success; as mentioned earlier, Harvard made the composition class the sole course required of all students in an otherwise elective curriculum. The teaching of writing was, as always, a cost-inefficient system when compared with other undergraduate courses. Attempts to keep these costs down were unsuccessful. Faculty at the University of Michigan in 1894, for example, understandably balked at a situation in which four teachers and two graduate assistants were responsible for 1,198 students. The situation at Harvard was better, with 20 teachers for 2,000 writing students, but not much better.[4]

The situation came to a head at Harvard in 1891. In seeking a solution to the difficulties of teaching writing, the Board of Overseers appointed a committee of three from outside the college, representatives of the world of affairs, to investigate English A, the required freshmen writing course.[5] These three men—Charles

Francis Adams, E. L. Godkin, and Josiah Quincy—with no training or experience in the teaching of writing, took the first and most important step toward shaping the teaching of writing at high schools and colleges for years to come.

The Committee took its task seriously, requesting English A teachers to submit a short theme from each of their students on the English training the students had received in preparatory school. They also examined entrance examinations written by students in 1892. The Committee members, disturbed by what they found, reproduced a few of the worst themes, some in facsimile as evidence of carelessness in handwriting and neatness. They concluded that the preparatory schools were failing and recommended that the schools immediately turn their attention to writing instruction in greater earnest. Learning to write was a responsibility of the lower schools. Colleges were to be concerned with more advanced skills. The solution was simple: Harvard should increase the standards of its entrance exam, excluding those who could not write.

The initial report was followed by an 1895 study of the translation of Latin and Greek in the lower schools and another in 1897 on freshman composition. The conclusions of both were the same as those of the original: the lower schools must do a better job of preparation. The Harvard Reports were widely publicized, bringing about a series of "Why Johnny Can't Write" articles in newspapers and magazines. Colleges across the country stiffened entrance exams. Everyone agreed that the deplorable situation was the fault of the secondary schools and should be corrected there. As has become the custom in America during such tempests, the schools were ordered to do a better job, but were given neither the money nor the techniques to do so. One beneficial effect, however, was that English instruction received more attention in secondary schools, fixing it permanently in the curriculum.

The larger effects of the Harvard Reports were unfortunate. Knowing nothing about writing instruction, the Committee members focused on the most obvious features of the essays they read, the errors in spelling, grammar, usage, and even handwriting. They thus gave support to the view that has haunted writing classes ever since: learning to write is learning matters of superficial correctness. They encouraged a conception of the composing process that found its way into the textbooks of two of the most influential figures in composition instruction in the late nineteenth century. And while Hill and Wendell never went as far as the Committee in restricting composing to correctness, the narrowness of the composing process they did recommend was in part due to its influence. Furthermore, the conspicuous position they occupied insured their success in promulgating a view that, as we shall see, defeated its better.

The Scientistic Approach

Current-traditional rhetoric as enunciated in the work of Hill, Wendell, and Genung arose in the last two decades of the nineteenth century, establishing a paradigm for teaching writing that has survived to the present. It was challenged at the time of its inception by Scott, Denney, and Buck, but not with any success, and it went virtually unquestioned until others took up the assault after 1960. Accepting the faculty psychology of eighteenth-century rhetoric, current-traditional rhetoric takes the most mechanical features of Campbell, Blair, and Whately and makes them the sole concern of the writing teacher. This view of writing instruction is also an extension of the elective system in the American college, with the various concerns included in eighteenth-century rhetoric relegated to their appropriate places in the college curriculum. From another point of view, it can be regarded as the manifestation of the assembly line in education. Current-traditional rhetoric is the triumph of the scientific and technical world view.

While the faculty psychology of eighteenth-century rhetoric is mechanical, locating reality in the external world, it is in its own way comprehensive, primarily because it attempts to take into account all features of human behavior—the sensory and rational, the ethical, and the aesthetic. We recall that Campbell, Blair, and Whately each considered persuasion to be the apotheosis of human art—or at least, in the case of Whately, of rhetoric—because it addressed itself to the total person: the emotions and the will, as well as the understanding, the reason, and the imagination. As I have repeatedly indicated, these faculties were mechanically conceived: they function independently of each other and they depend upon sensory experience; they are receptacles or muscles or malleable surfaces brought into play by experience. They do not shape experience, but are shaped by it. Still, all are considered necessary to the rhetorical act, even if all are not involved at any one time.

Current-traditional rhetoric, on the other hand, accepts this mechanistic faculty psychology, but removes ethical and all but the most elementary emotional considerations from the concern of rhetoric. Rhetoric's sole appeal is to the understanding and reason, with its highest manifestation to be found in exposition and argument. The distinction between argument—the bringing about of conviction through appeals to the reason—and persuasion—appealing to the will through emotion in order to bring about action— is accepted. Persuasion, however, is made the province of oratory and is relegated to speech departments. The appeals to imagination and emotion found in poetry are consigned to the literature section of the English department. The business of the composition teacher is to train the remaining faculties, and despite the attention paid to argument, this effort focuses primarily on the understanding, the faculty involved in scientific investigation. Exposition, "setting forth" what is inductively discovered (narration and description are similary conceived), becomes the central concern of writing classes. This is also, of course, the kind of writing most valued by the technologically oriented business community. Freshman English becomes a course in technical writing.

This scheme severely restricts the composing process. The writer's duty is to rid himself of the trappings of culture that distort his perceptions. He is to be objective, detached, in observing experience. The purpose of writing is to report, not interpret, what is inductively discovered. Reality surrenders its meaning readily when correctly approached, with the proper detachment. Invention is not necessary: after all, the scientist does not invent meaning, he discovers it through the correct use of his method. The job of composing is to find the language that corresponds to the observed phenomena. Sign and thing are arbitrarily connected, and the writer's task is to select the sign that best captures, and contains, the thing-in-itself. Teaching the student to do so—teaching style—is the real purpose of a writing course, since the rest is prescribed by the scientific method, or the method of the discipline the student is pursuing, most commonly, of course, the scientific one. The audience is not important since all that is asked of the writer is to affect the appropriate faculty, reproducing the original experience in the minds of the reader. The auditor has no part in the shaping of meaning. The writer's job is to concentrate on the experience itself, the source of meaning, and the language that best translates the experience, not on the audience.

In the rest of the chapter, I would like to trace the development of this narrowing of the province of composition to exposition, with its concentration on style, during the last 30 years of the century. With the increase in students, a host of textbooks appeared, each in its own way trying to define the purview of rhetoric in the new curriculum. I should say at the start that I will be relying on the survey of materials offered in Kitzhaber's extraordinary dissertation on the period, although the conclusions reached are my own, based on an examination of the same materials. My main focus will be an analysis of the redefining of the composing process as it is shaped by the new scientific rhetoric.

Before I examine the development of current-traditional rhetoric, it will be useful to survey the field as a whole. The definition of rhetoric that persisted was a simplification of Campbell's adaptation construction, emphasizing that the writer's aim is to bring about a particular effect on the audience. As I have already indicated, the audience is passive and static, not contributing to the shaping of meaning. The *invention* of discovery of classical rhetoric is replaced by a managerial invention, taking the shape of the forms of discourse—description, narration, exposition, and argument. Rhetoric, it is asserted, cannot teach the discovery of the content of discourse, but it can teach students to manage it, once found, so that it appeals to the appropriate faculty. This new invention is thus made a part of arrangement. Since language must be chosen to embody the content of thought, the study of diction and sentence structure becomes an abiding concern, both resting on eighteenth-century theories of language.

Invention

The discussion of invention in textbooks of the last half of the nineteenth century has caused considerable confusion.[6] Almost all textbooks use the term, either to deny that it is a part of rhetoric or to explain what role it plays in the composing process. Both groups, however, go on to present a managerial view of invention, agreeing that the actual discovery of material is outside the composing process, and providing advice for managing that which is available. Thus, E. O. Haven in *Rhetoric: A Textbook* (1869), T. W. Hunt in *Principles of Written Discourse* (1884), and D. J. Hill in *Science of Rhetoric* (1877), all explicitly agree with the position of Adams Sherman Hill: "Being the art of communication by *language*, Rhetoric applies to any subject-matter that can be treated in words, but has no subject-matter peculiar to itself. It does not undertake to furnish a person with something to say; but it does undertake to tell him how best to say that which he has provided himself."[7] On the other hand, Henry Day in *Art of Discourse* (1850, 1867), James DeMille in *Elements of Rhetoric* (1878), and John Franklin Genung in *Practical Elements of Rhetoric* (1885) insist on invention as the center of rhetoric.

When these textbooks are examined, however, we see that all treat invention as the office of presenting the message so as to affect the reader in the manner intended. The effect on the audience, rather than the discourse, is the determiner of inventional strategies. Consequently, all divide discourse into forms, according to the faculty which is to be addressed. The forms of discourse have a long and rich history, originating in Campbell and formalized in the nineteenth century by Alexander Bain.[8] Regardless of the exact content of the forms chosen, however, they are based on a mechanistic faculty psychology, assuming that one faculty can dominate in the kind of appeal made by the discourse, and in the audience's response to it. Thus, the inventional devices offered in textbooks in the last part of the century consist of advice on shaping the message so that it will act on the appropriate faculty.

This managerial invention is found everywhere, but most tellingly for later textbooks in Genung and A. S. Hill. The second part of Genung's *Practical Elements of Rhetoric* is entitled "Invention." After explaining that invention is a natural gift that can be cultivated by habits of observation, thought, and reading, he presents chapters on outlining, on using the thoughts of others, and the following:

IV   Invention dealing with Observed Objects: Description
V   Invention dealing with Events: Narration
VI   Invention dealing with Generalizations: Exposition
VII   Invention dealing with Truths: Argumentation
VIII Invention dealing with Practical Issues: Persuasion[9]

Invention involves shaping the subject matter so that it appeals to the right faculty, the faculty selected rising inevitably out of the subject matter. A. S. Hill's *Principles of Rhetoric* also devotes its second half to the forms: description, narration, exposition, and argument. Because of their continuous influence—even today—both schemes merit close examination.

I said before that current-traditional rhetoric reduces the composing act to a concern for exposition—for "setting forth" the rational and empirical in an appeal to the reason and understanding. This is obvious everywhere in Genung. Writers use description and narration in the "effort to report what they observe in the world around them." While Genung admits that description portrays "concrete objects, material or spiritual, by means of language," [10] he is obviously more concerned with the material, giving only two pages to the use of metaphor to suggest "those objects which appeal not to the reader's sense-perception but to his consciousness of his own inner experience." [11] Narration is likewise seen as "the recounting, in succession, of the particulars that make up a transaction," [12] with the emphasis once again on external events. In both cases, Genung—still a belletrist—completes the discussion by briefly indicating the use of description and narration in poetic products. While these matters are not his main concern, they are perfectly consistent with what precedes, since they follow Blair in offering an eighteenth-century poetic in keeping with the eighteenth-century rhetoric.

Description and narration deal with particulars of sense impression while exposition bases itself on these for the purpose of "exhibiting ideas, as generalized in the mind." Exposition is responsible for "*setting forth the meaning of things*; and this we may regard as its fundamental office. It is not concerned primarily with establishing the truth or falsity of a thing; it seeks rather what the thing *is*,—what is its real nature, its scope, its relations." It is here and in the section on argumentation that the modes of exposition are offered. Thus, through the back door, the topics of invention are introduced, but now in the service of science: "From the perception of individual things, the mind readily advances to the thought of classes of things: detecting throughout the world resemblances and contrasts, laws and principles, causes and effects; it begins to group things together, to generalize, to discover qualities essential and qualities accidental, to form, in a word, scientific conceptions of things."[13] Genung concerns himself with these topics in dealing with exposition and argumentation, the latter adapted in simplified form from Whately. Argumentation is nothing more than an extension of exposition, since its function is twofold: "either to set the truth directly before the mind and adduce facts and arguments to substantiate it; or to attack some erroneous position which, being demolished, will leave the truth in question free to assert itself."[14] Truth is self-evident.

Genung treats persuasion in a way that removes it from the composition classroom. Genung at first appears to be following Campbell, but finally regards writing in a light that substantially limits its scope. Agreeing with Campbell, Genung looks upon persuasion as the apotheosis of rhetoric. Since it affects the will of the speaker, "it has the highest object, [and] must seek to enlist all the spiritual powers, imparting alike thought, emotion, and impulse"—in short, all the faculties.[15] Persuasion, however, cannot be undertaken without "the close contact of personal presence." It "presupposes a speaker at close quarters with his audience."[16] This insistence on the oral act removes persuasion from a place in Genung's rhetoric, leaving to the composition class the scientific use of language. In subsequent textbooks, Genung either omits persuasion altogether or gives it scant attention.

I have focused first on Genung in demonstrating the place of an *inventio* of management in the new, scientific rhetoric because he is the most thorough in his statement of it. The same limitation of invention is found in A. S. Hill in an earlier and equally influential textbook. In *Principles of Rhetoric*, we find the same narrow empiricism and the appeals to the various faculties, each operating in isolation from the others. Description brings "before the mind of the reader persons or things as they appear to the writer."[17] Narration is similar but it shows persons and things in action. Exposition is explanation, but it "does not address the imagination, the feelings, or the will. It addresses the understanding exclusively, and it may deal with any subject-matter with which the understanding has to do."[18] Argument, Hill explains, "like exposition, addresses the understanding,"[19] but it leads to belief rather than understanding. Persuasion is treated as a subclass of argument, differing from its source in that it "is addressed not so much to the intellect as to the feelings."[20] It is relegated to the status of a "useful adjunct,"[21] and is presented briefly, almost as an afterthought, with little enthusiasm. It has obviously fallen in Hill's scheme. Furthermore, in his *Foundations of Rhetoric* of 1892, he turns his back on the modes altogether, focusing on words, sentences, and paragraphs, further limiting the scope of composition instruction.

As Kitzhaber has demonstrated, there were voices contributing to the dominance of the four forms of discourse in the textbooks that appeared after 1890—for example, Arlo Bates' *Talks on Writing English, First Series* (1896) agreeing with Genung and Hill and C. S. Baldwin's *College Manual of Rhetoric* (1902) disagreeing with them.[22] But the pattern established by Genung and Hill prevailed, with persuasion removed from the forms of written discourse and the remainder simplified.

There was one other notable attempt to provide students with something to say in writing classes—the composition topic. Assigning a subject for student essays originated with Roman rhetoric, but in the eighties and nineties it was given renewed attention. The topics offered were intended to appeal to the students, growing out of personal experience. On the face of it, this seems a new development, one in keeping with an Emersonian rhetoric. In practice, however, these topics were commonly based on the forms of discourse. Genung, for instance, assigned topics appropriate to the forms in order of difficulty—description, narration, exposition, and argumentation—arguing that these proceeded from the most elementary faculties to the most complex.[23] These composition topics, furthermore, tended to encourage either close observation, in the scientific sense, or the use of research materials, the thinking of others. In both cases, the student was again asked to report on what was external to him, either empirical data or the work of better observers than he himself.

Arrangement

The managerial scheme of invention made arrangement, through the forms of discourse, central. There were, however, two other areas in which current-traditional rhetoric addressed the problem of arrangement: the paragraph and the principles of unity, coherence, and emphasis.

Teaching the paragraph as the center of the composition course came into vogue in the nineties.[24] Once again, Alexander Bain, the

Scottish rhetorician, was the first to discuss the subject systematically. Having studied actual paragraphs, Bain prescribed a set of six rules: (1) Each sentence must be related to that which preceded it; (2) Parallel thought must employ parallel structure; (3) The first sentence of a paragraph should indicate the subject; (4) Each sentence should be appropriately situated in the paragraph; (5) The paragraph must display unity; and (6) Principal and subordinate parts must be appropriately arranged. The rules offered were generally sane, but they were, once again, based on the expository paragraph, the form appropriate to scientific rhetoric. Bain also tended to look upon the six rules as principles without exception, as did those who followed him in their use in the classroom.

One of the most influential followers of Bain in America was A. D. Hepburn, the first to argue that the paragraph was "a discussion in miniature,"[25] and that its principles of arrangement were the same as that of the essay as a whole. D. J. Hill carried this a step further, offering several patterns of paragraph development, including definition, contrast, illustration, and others. (Once again, the Aristotelian commonplaces were tapped to become a device for arrangement.) After 1880, almost all textbooks followed this example in greater or lesser degree. In the nineties, when the daily theme became common, largely as a result of the Harvard Reports and the example of Barrett Wendell, the notion that a paragraph was an essay in miniature became highly popular. After all, evaluating an essay a day—or correcting it, as was more commonly the case —could be impossibly time consuming. Fred Newton Scott and Joseph Villiers Denney did much to promote this practice in *Paragraph-Writing*. They were especially influential in encouraging the writing of paragraphs according to the forms of discourse: exposition, argumentation, description, and narration. Unfortunately, their attempt to introduce an organic notion of the paragraph failed, while their codification of nineteenth-century thinking on the paragraph has stood until just recently.

The appearance of unity, coherence, and emphasis as principles of arrangement is closely related to the development of interest in the paragraph. Earlier forms of the three can be traced—first seen in Blair, developed by Bain, and then presented in a variety of ways by textbooks between 1870 and the end of the century.[26] Barrett Wendell used the three in the form that finally caught on. A number of textbook writers, most notably A. S. Hill, had argued that the principles involved in the construction of sentences could be applied to the paragraph. Wendell extended the application to the essay as a whole. In an attempt to simplify writing instruction in his freshmen classes, Wendell argued that the principles of composition in the sentence and of arrangement in the paragraph and larger units of discourse could be reduced to three: unity, coherence, and mass—the last eventually becoming emphasis in the hands of others. At the level of the sentence and word there is always a conflict between these three qualities, on the one hand, and good use, on the other—good use being Wendell's major concern. In the whole composition, however, good use is of little help to the student, so that unity, coherence, and mass become the major concerns.

In actual composing, the principles are of little use. Wendell assumed that the student would know what he wanted to say so that the only concern was with arrangement. This too is not difficult because the structure of the discourse should follow the order of thought, a mere duplication of the rationally or empirically real. Given the certainty of these matters, instruction in arrangement can be organized around the three principles: "(1) Every composition should group itself about one central idea; (2) The chief part of every composition should be so placed as readily to catch the eye; (3) Finally, the relation of each part of a composition to its neighbors should be unmistakable."[27] It is difficult to disagree with this, but how it will help the student to write is an unresolved matter.

Style

The consideration of unity, coherence, and emphasis is an appropriate introduction to the focal point of current-traditional rhetoric. The emergence of these principles, as well as the attention to the paragraph, was an extension of Blair's treatment of style. Blair was attempting to discover what in rhetoric was reducible to rule, and American textbooks between 1870 and 1900 applied his stylistic dictates to the structure of the discourse as a whole, as well as to all its parts, adding in the process Campbell's and Whately's advice on the word and sentence. Composition textbooks during the period were commonly arranged in order of the word, the sentence, the arrangement of larger units—the paragraph and the whole composition—and the forms of discourse.[28] Style was thought to be the main concern of textbooks—offered along with the forms of discourse—because it could be reduced to a set of abstract principles, succinctly stated. Since the matter of discourse had been discovered outside rhetoric, arrangement and expression became the main concerns. Experience is inherently arranged in orderly patterns, the forms being simple aids to recording them. This leaves style, here conceived as the matching of sign to nonverbal reality. As mentioned earlier, A. S. Hill's *Foundations of Rhetoric* (1892), his second textbook, ignores the forms altogether, focusing on words, sentences, and paragraphs. Barrett Wendell's *English Composition* (1891) does not mention the forms at all, devoting itself to writing as style, "the expression of thought and feeling in written words."[29] Their narrow conception of rhetoric was not atypical.

Blair, Campbell, and Whately had all listed qualities of style to be sought in writing and speaking. Blair had discussed purity, precision, clearness, strength, unity, and harmony. Campbell considered purity, perspicuity, vivacity, elegance, animation, and music. Whately simplified the list, discussing perspicuity, energy, and elegance. All, however, were arguing from the perspective of a mechanistic epistemology, looking upon words as carrying force or energy in varying degrees, to be used to "strengthen the impression which we seek to make."[30] Signs are capable of assuming the character of the experience they represent, so that some are better than others in impressing upon the mind (literally) the qualities of their referents. Thus, all three emphasize the concrete term over the abstract since it is closer to actual sensory experience, the basis of all knowledge.

As long as theoretical considerations were included in textbooks, the relationship between the advice on style given and its reason for being was clear. In American textbooks after 1870, however, this theoretical apparatus was dropped, and the rationale for the principles offered was lost. Textbook authors still recommended the abstract principles of the old order. Hill and Wendell, for example, insisted on clearness, force, and elegance, and Genung on clearness, force, and beauty. Other texts, influenced by Herbert Spencer, introduced economy.[31] Without their explicit grounding in a mechanistic epistemology, however, this advice seemed arbitrary, even though it was offered in the most authoritative of tones. Still, from one point of view, these principles were serving their original purpose, since they were used to tacitly support a scientific world view.

A discussion of figurative language was also included in many textbooks of the eighties and nineties. These were again based on Blair and Campbell, arguing for figures as ornamentation, mere mechanical devices added to thought in order to communicate rational or empirical truths more effectively. Eventually, these discussions were dropped from composition texts as literature courses appropriated this area of rhetoric.[32] The result was a further limiting of the province of the writing course, focusing on the use of language in a way appropriate to science and technology.

Usage and, later, grammar were deep and abiding concerns of composition books during this time. As Walter J. Ong has demonstrated, Latin had long been used as the language of the educated, placing an indelible mark on those who had attained the highest culture.[33] In the last third of the nineteenth century, classical languages in American universities were no longer required. The elective system had made them just one of the numerous options available to students. As I have already mentioned, however, the same was not true of freshman composition. Harvard long maintained it as the sole requirement for all students, and the Harvard Reports made the ability to write correctly, if not necessarily with intelligence, an important rite in the entrance process for college. The mark of the educated was now the use of a certain version of the native language, a version that tended to coincide with the dialect of the upper middle class, the group that had customarily attended college. Children of the lower orders were now asked to prove their worthiness for a place in the upper ranks of society—now defined by profession as well as income—by learning this dialect. Composition teachers became the caretakers of the English tongue, and more important, the gatekeepers on the road to the good things in life, as defined by the professional class.[34]

Most composition textbooks adopted Campbell's prescriptions on diction: it must be reputable, present, and national. Campbell had written at a time when the middle class was on the ascent, and so his adoption in American colleges during this period is not surprising. A. S. Hill uses Campbell's offenses against grammatical purity in the first book of his *Principles*, discussing barbarisms, improprieties, and solecisms. We have already seen that Wendell looked upon style as a tension between good use and unity, mass, and coherence. Genung included accurate use, present use, intelligible use, and scholarly use—again a variation of Campbell. These discussions of usage were authoritative in tone and frequently arbitrary, imposing standards that are clearly dialectal biases of a particular class. The authors, however, assume the voice of expert witnesses, reporting on certain and irrefutable matters. All seem to be striving for the conviction of the scientist, unconscious that they are reporting a class bias, not a physical law.

Grammar did not first appear in college-level texts, knowledge of it being assumed as a condition of college entrance.[35] With the admission of working-class students to the college, however, grammar instruction found its way into writing courses. The sentence diagram, for example, first appeared in Alonzo Reed and Brainerd Kellogg's *Higher Lessons in English* in 1878. Handbooks began to appear as supplements to the regular text, and more lengthy discussions of grammatical matters were included in the text itself. The grammar vogue subsided in the nineties as paragraph instruction and the daily theme became the center of the classroom. Colleges also at this time invoked the Harvard Reports in placing responsibility for grammar instruction on the lower schools. Instruction in grammar at the college level, however, was revived at around the turn of the century. Unfortunately, the grammar used was an eighteenth-century construction, its proponents remaining totally oblivious to the work of linguists being carried on in the same departments as were the composition courses.

The Consequences

By the end of the century, the typical composition textbook was devoted to the forms of discourse, stylistic matters organized around the principles of unity, coherence, and emphasis, and discussions of usage and grammar. Superficial correctness had become the most significant measure of accomplished prose. These textbooks were designed to serve the professional aspirations of the middle class, and those who would be of the middle class. There was an avowed commitment to the "practical," with the term itself appearing in many of the new titles. This meant, the authors explained, that the course was to be organized around actual writing, not the memorization of rhetorical principles as in earlier texts. The stress on the practical also meant activities useful in the professional world, in the realm of scientific technology. Genung, for example, explained that he had introduced the "laboratory method" in the writing class. Students were to learn to write by studying literary models, especially the informal essay, discovering their stylistic principles for themselves and then applying them in their own composing.[36] He was obviously trying to emulate the method of his colleagues in the new science departments. Genung's method also produced the first of the freshman anthologies, soon to become ubiquitous in beginning writing classes, combining the positivistic epistemology of the rhetoric text with an eighteenth-century belletristic aesthetic. (Many anthologies continue to do so.) Wendell encouraged the daily theme, a journal entry of 100 words or so on a topic drawn from personal observation. The method encouraged writing and saved the student and teacher time (time, after all, is money) in preparing for class. He even encouraged student editorial groups, charging them with the task of seeking out errors in superficial correctness, once again introducing efficiency.[37] Since classes continued to be large, correction symbols were introduced, an effective way for managing large numbers of essays more quickly.[38] Textbooks in general became shorter, as the center of the writing class became the study of informal essays, short poems, and short stories; the writing of themes; and the correction of themes by the teacher. Students were being told less and less about composing and were being asked to write more and more.

While it would at first seem unfair to fault a system that teaches writing by having students write, the disappointing feature of this method appears in the view of composing being taught. If textbooks told students anything about the stages of composing, they provided a mechanical model. The student was to select the subject, narrow it to a thesis, make an outline of the essay, write the essay, and edit it for correctness.[39] They might also be given suggestions for introductions and conclusions. While the student was often told to adapt his message to the audience, he was given no instructions for doing so, or he was given an abstract model of audience response based on the old faculty psychology and the forms of discourse. This conception is a clear example of Whately revisited—a view of composing grounded in a positivist epistemology. The best that can be said of this model is that students were indeed writing. The worst that can be said is that this model severely restricts the student's response to experience. Current-traditional rhetoric dictates that certain matters cannot be discussed because they are either illusory—not empirically verifiable—or they cannot be contained within acceptable structures—rational categories, for example. This very exclusion, meanwhile, encourages a mode of behavior that helps students in their move up the corporate ladder—correctness in usage, grammar, clothing, thought, and a certain sterile objectivity and disinterestedness.

After 1900, current-traditional rhetoric became entrenched in the college curriculum. The attention that had been paid to writing instruction by academics and the business community simultaneously ceased. Composition teachers were no longer important figures in the new university, as they had been when Hill, Wendell, and Scott found an audience for their book-length statements on the teaching of writing. Wendell and Genung, for example, turned their attention to literary criticism, as did the best of the new graduate students and college teachers. Composition courses continued as permanent fixtures in English departments, partly because they were demanded by professional schools who were in touch with the demands made on their students in the business world, partly because freshman English helped finance less profitable parts of department offerings. Literary studies became the intellectual center of English departments, providing the road to advancement in the newly formed profession of college teaching, now as rigorously organized as the best corporations. Composition instruction became apprenticeship work, left to graduate students and junior faculty members. Rhetoric and poetic were hopelessly divided, writing teachers remaining in the eighteenth century while their colleagues in literature remained open to new ideas. This was in part due to the emergence of the new research-oriented university, defining faculty members as scholars and trainers of new scholars in graduate schools. Undergraduate education in the university system was given low priority, and it was the new universities that trained the teachers now entering the profession. Of equal importance, freshman English, with its positivist epistemology, was probably doing an adequate job of training students for the new technical professions, encouraging a view of reality that held them in good stead in their professional lives.[40] Finally, no large influx of students to universities—no substantial broadening of the middle class—occurred until after World War II, when an expanding economy meant that new students entered the universities, to be trained for new jobs, awakening once gain the interest of the business community in writing competency.

7

An Alternative Voice:
Fred Newton Scott

THE RHETORIC OF FRED NEWTON SCOTT REPRESENTS A NEW DI-
rection for college writing instruction. Scott was struggling to for-
mulate a new pedagogical paradigm, one that was distinctively
American in its conception, addressing the problems peculiar to
communicating in a democratic society. His intellectual origins can
be traced to Emerson, but he was operating within the philosophical structure of American Pragmatism, especially as found in William James and the early John Dewey. At every turn, Scott was consciously formulating an alternative to current-tradtional rhetoric,
particularly its scientific epistemology and its class bias. Unfortunately, Scott was defeated, and were it not for the efforts of Donald Stewart to reclaim him as part of our intellectual heritage, he
would be unknown today.[1] One reason for his neglect can be traced
to the textbooks he published, along with Joseph Villiers Denney
and Gertrude Buck. These only suggest the originality of his contribution, in part because he had been subjected to the pressures of
the marketplace, on more than one occasion altering a textbook at
the urging of his publishers.[2] The real strength of his thinking is instead found in the statements he made about rhetoric and the composing process in the prefaces to his textbooks and in other publications, as well as in the comments of his collaborators and students.

Scott's intellectual roots are in Emerson, but his thought most
commonly bears the marks of American Pragmatism. (It might almost be said that Emerson's rhetoric as I earlier described it becomes a basis for a metaphysic in Pragmatism.)[3] For Scott, reality is

a social construction, a creation emerging from the dialectical interplay of individuals using language in order to survive in a world bounded by the material. Reality is neither exclusively external, as for Common Sense Realism, nor is it exclusively internal, as for philosophical idealism. Instead, it is the result of the interaction between the experience of the external world and what the perceiver brings to this experience. The relations that bring about reality, however, also include the social, the interaction of human beings. The medium of contact between the perceiver and perceived is language. Language, however, is not a simple system in which sign and thought are matched up. It is constitutive of reality, the very condition of thought. Language does not exist apart from thought and thought does not exist apart from language: they are one and the same. It is clear how this scheme is inherently rhetorical. Reality is constituted by the interplay of observer (writer or speaker), other observer (audience), and language. The product of this dialectic is reality.

Perhaps the best place to start in examining Scott's rhetoric is found in his statements about language. In "English Composition as a Mode of Behavior" (1922), Scott attacks the destruction of the student's desire to communicate by the methods used to teach writing, especially the brutality of theme correction. For Scott, students bring with them to school the inherent ability to use language: "It is a mode of behavior like leaping, running, or tossing the arms. Words to a child are wishes, commands, ways of securing what one wants, ways of piercing out gestures."[4] Scott explains: "When the child enters the school he is possessed, therefore, of two invaluable gifts: an eagerness to communicate and be communicated with, and a vocabulary—if we may stretch the term to include all significant externalizings of himself—sufficient to convey his feelings and his ideas to his playmates."[5] Teachers respond to this linguistic competence by forcing "the clash between, on the one hand, the instinctive, inherited impulse to communication, and, on the other hand, the scholastic system of abstract symbolism which, under the name of language studies, grammar, and rhetoric, we now use in the schools and regard as indispensable as a medium of culture."[6] Scott's description of the phenomenon reveals his awareness of the loyalties of the camp he is opposing, the mechanistic view of the mind as container or muscle: "And now upon this seething caldron [*sic*] of commuicative impulses, the school, as ordinarily conducted, clamps the lid of linguistic ritual. The teacher approaches the pupil as if he were a great emptiness to be filled and a great dumbness to be made vocal." Sounding like Piaget, Scott explains that the child's language is concrete and specific, but the school requires that he perform in the area of the abstact. This new language is different in degree only, not in kind, but it is offered as superior in all respects, giving "a pretense—of unity, symmetry, order, and restraint that was conspicuously absent in the other."[7] The student's language, growing naturally out of an inherent desire to communicate in a social setting, is declared useless in carrying out genuine communication. Theme writing in all its lifeless abstraction is set up as the standard.

Scott does not deny the value of the abstract in educating the child. What he does attack is the insistence on the abstract—a Cartesian rationality—at the expense of the concrete language of the child. The frightful errors students display in writing essays are "the outward signs of an inward lesion—of the disjunction of two phases of man's nature that can work as they should only when they work together."[8] What is needed is the dialectical interplay of the concrete and abstract: sensory impression—the strength of the child—with the abstract organizing principles taught in schools. Furthermore, these organizing principles must not be exclusively scientific or rational, but products of the social environment:

> If the disorders that I have described are due to dissociation, the remedy lies in bringing the dissociated things together, that is, (1) in finding in the impulse to untrammeled communication, in spite of its seeming waywardness, the vague beginnings of a sense for unity, for symmetry, for restraint, for proportion, and attaching to these vague feelings the simplest aspects of the symbolic apparatus; and (2) in introducing into the symbolic apparatus the ideas of sociability and quick communication belonging to the other phase, of which it is now usually devoid.[9]

The danger of failing to ground education in the social experience of the child is not simply bad writing. It leads to the denial of significant areas of human experience—experience that cannot be expressed in what Scott calls elsewhere the language of the schoolmaster. Language is experience and experience is language: to deny the student the language of his experience is to deny the possibility of considering the experience, or even of continuing to enjoy it. The child is invalidated. Thus, Scott approvingly quotes Renan on the limits of the French language: "The French care only to express that which is clear. As it happens, the most important truths, those that relate to the transformation of life, are not clear; one only perceives them in a kind of half-light."[10]

This essay is a remarkable statement. Scott has summarized the significance of Emerson's thought on language, without the super-structure of philosophical idealism. Earlier, Gertrude Buck, a stu-dent of Scott and then a collaborator, had applied a variation of Emerson's theory of metaphor to rhetoric.[11] Both Scott and Buck throughout rely on view of reality as a linguistic construct arising out of a social act, an interaction among communicator, audience, and language.

Scott further displays the influence of Emerson in his definition of rhetoric. In "The Two Ideals of Composition Teaching," he presents a thumbnail sketch of the history of rhetoric, setting up two dominant camps. The first owes its origin to the Sicilian, Korax, and to Aris-totle. This is a rhetoric whose sole purpose is success: "Whether the speaker's cause was right or wrong, whether justice was being pro-moted or defeated, was no business of the teacher."[12] With an ob-vious reference to current-traditional rhetoric, Scott explains that this is still the prevailing scheme, "nothing more than a system of verbal tricks to hold the reader's attention or to titillate his literary palate."[13] Against this rhetoric he places that of Plato, who offers a "strict adherence to the truth; for the ideal of success at any cost he substitutes the ideal of self-sacrificing devotion to the interest of the community. To say only what we believe to be true and what we think will be helpful to our fellow-men, is the end and aim, accord-ing to Plato, of instruction in this noble art."[14] This appears to be an Emersonian reading of Plato, placing rhetoric at the center of a democratic society, making it the response of the total individual— ethical as well as rational—acting within a language community. Scott confirms this view in "The Standard of American Speech." As an appropriate standard to guide us in pronunciation, he points to a passage from Whitman: "The charm of the beautiful pronunciation of all words, of all tongues, is in perfect flexible vocal organs and in a developed harmonious soul." Scott then adds:

If this doctrine is true, the stuff out of which a great national language is created is the simple, homely expression of sincere feeling and sturdy thinking. Live nobly, think good thoughts, have right feelings, be genuine, do not scream or strain to make pretense, cultivate a harmonious soul—follow these injunctions, and you are laying the foundation of a standard of American speech. Whence the speech comes does not matter. It may be the language of Potash and Perlmutter. It may be composed of all the dialects spoken in Chicago or in San Francisco. It may be the speech of Boston, of Texas, or of Montana. No matter. If it is the voice of high wisdom, of moderation, of human nature at its best, the words will take on that power and charm which is the test of a great national speech.[15]

Rhetoric, in theory and practice, must be based on a holistic response, involving the total person, the ethical and aesthetic as well as the rational. The rhetoric that insists on the language of a particular class demands that all experience conform to the limits of a particular class, in the process denying the wholeness of the human response. The result of this exclusiveness, Scott realized, was a rhetoric of success, not truth, and the alienation of the individual from his culture and himself.

After considering Scott's theoretical statements about rhetoric, his textbooks are a bit disappointing. There we find the familiar emphasis on diction, sentence, style, the paragraph, and the forms of discourse. This emphasis is undoubtedly due, in part, to the pressures of the marketplace, as mentioned earlier. An equally plausible explanation is that Scott had not yet translated his ideas into classroom practice. He admits in "English Composition as a Mode of Behavior," for example, that he had not yet found a simple solution to the dissociation of concrete and abstract language he described. He was also in part limited by the psychological theory of his day—the work of G. Stanley Hall and Edward Lee Thorndike,[16] for example—which led him to narrow his Emersonian vision in the direction of mechanistic thinking. Still, much of what he offers in these textbooks is refreshing in its concept of the composing process.

Although a great deal of what appears in Scott's textbooks is also found in current-traditional rhetoric—the forms of discourse, the paragraph, and the like—it is always made distinct by the insistence on the rhetorical context. Scott and his collaborators repeatedly assert the necessity of placing communication within a framework demanding that the student consider the relationships among the writer or speaker, the subject considered, and the audience. In *New Composition-Rhetoric*, Scott and Denney assert that writing and speaking are social acts. In *Elementary English Composition* they explain this in detail: "The forces which urge young persons to express themselves with tongue or pen are partly individual, partly social,—partly impulses from within, partly solicitations from without. Pupils compose most naturally and most successfully when the two forces are in equilibrium."[17] Scott and Denney offer an alternative that places even correctness in a new context: "Presented as a means of meeting definite social needs more or less effectively, of winning attention and consideration, the various devices of grammar and rhetoric make an appeal to self-interest which pupils can understand." Students learn grammar and usage because they come to "appreciate the value of these things to themselves as members of society."[18]

This emphasis on the social value of rhetoric is related to another departure from current-traditional rhetoric. Scott and Denney wish to reunite spoken and written discourse. Spoken discourse is valuable training for the writer because it involves an actual audience, requiring the student to shape his message for a particular social gathering of individuals. It insists that the interlocutor consider others—in their variety and uniqueness—in the communication act. This in turn improves writing, teaching the student to respond to his audience not as a set of abstract faculties, but as whole human beings. The reunion of speaking and writing also does much to put persuasion back into the rhetoric class, demanding as it does a more comprehensive response.

Although *Elementary English Composition* devotes two-thirds of its content to the four modes, oral and written, it presents them differently because of the kinds of writing assignments given the student. In the third number of *Contributions to Rhetorical Theory*, edited by Scott, Denney explains the principles the two used in drawing up topics:

> If our object is to train the power of seeing and expressing relations, of grasping in imagination the meaning and total significance of a number of details, the statement of the topics should, if possible, suggest a typical

situation in real life. And if we wish to enlist the personal interest of the writer in his work, the statement of the topics should suggest a personal relationship to the situation, of the one who is to write. Moreover it should suggest a particular reader or set of readers who are to be brought into vital relationship with the situation. . . . The composition that suggests a problem or solution calls into activity all of the resources of the pupil.[19]

At a time when students were given vague directives to write about a work of literature or about what "interested" them, Scott and Denney were offering students a complete rhetorical situation that arose out of their experience, including the purpose of the writer, his role, and the audience to be addressed. And every feature of writing instruction—grammar, usage, paragraphs, forms of discourse—was offered within this rhetorical context. Literary topics were included, but they too were placed within a rhetorical frame considering purpose and audience in interpretation.

It should be emphasized that Scott and Denney were not simply recommending adapting the message to the audience. Current-traditional rhetoric sees meaning as external to the composing process, and the auditor as a set of discrete faculties, each faculty a button to be pushed when appropriate to the effect intended. This is why specific audiences are not named: they are not a part of the meaning-making process. For Scott and Denney, meaning arises out of the interaction of the interlocutor and the audience. The significance of a work of literature will be different, for example, according to the person to whom it is being explained. Truth is contextual, depending on perspective and setting. In her treatise on metaphor, Buck thus argues that any theory based exclusively on self-expression or exclusively on audience effect is one-sided: communication in poetry involves an interaction of both.[20]

The essential difference between Scott and current-traditionalists can be seen in the metaphors that govern each. As I have repeatedly shown, current-traditional rhetoric is governed by the image of the machine. The observer carefully notes the effects of sense impression and the faculties set in motion by these impressions. He then tries to set up the same mental operations in the auditor, reporting the experience as closely as possible to its original. The process is linear in time and space, increment added to increment. The metaphor guiding Scott's rhetoric is that of the plant. Meaning grows, with a variety of mental operations occurring simultaneously, as the perceiver, a unique whole, brings all of his past experiences to the particular situation. This situation includes not only the writer and the issue being considered, but the audience to be involved in the communication situation. The meaning that arises is never totally predictable because it is never simply the sum of the parts making it up. In short, truth grows out of the rhetorical act: it is not imposed from without. Buck makes this explicit. Traditional rhetoric, she says, looks upon metaphor as a mechanism, "like a box, whose parts, gathered from different sources are put together to make a whole." Metaphor is instead, "the result of a vital process, more like a plant or animal, whose members grow from the same source, out of a homogenous mass into a clearly differentiated structure."[21] Similarly, in *Composition-Rhetoric, Designed for Use in Secondary Schools*, Scott and Denney explain: "A third idea which underlies the work is the idea of growth. A composition is regarded not as a dead form, to be analyzed into its component parts, but as a living product of an active, creative mind. The paragraph is compared to a plant, springing up in the soil of the mind from a germinal idea, and the course of its development, assuming naturally a variety of forms."[22] Unfortunately, the notion of growth found in Scott, Denney, and Buck is often itself mechanical, influenced by the positivism of their biological and psychological models of human behavior. Still, their conception of an organic composing process is superior to that found in current-traditional rhetoric, if only because it tries to restore ethical and aesthetic considerations to rhetoric, making composing a process that involves a holistic response to experience.

The rhetoric of Scott, Denney, and Buck did not prevail. As far as college composition is concerned, it disappeared. Still, the debate that they began continued, now fought in the public schools. Scott, along with G. R. Carpenter and F. T. Baker, had in 1903 published *The Teaching of English in the Elementary and Secondary School*, and he was throughout his career concerned with English education in the schools. His ideas, if not his name, were thus kept alive as one of the voices in the continuing discussion of the teaching of writing to schoolchildren,[23] ready to be called upon by university composition teachers when they were once again ripe for them.

8

Postscript on the Present

AT THE END OF THE NINETEENTH CENTURY, COMPOSITION
courses became firmly established in the new American college.
And although these courses have since undergone periodic assaults
from teachers, administrators, and students,[1] they remain one of the
few permanent features of the college curriculum. The freshman
writing course has somehow managed to prove itself indispensable
to a student's education. While there are, doubtless, numerous and
complicated reasons for this fact, one obvious explanation is that the
student's ability to use language effectively is perhaps the single
most important result of a college education. As I have tried to
show, the way in which students are taught to use language—the
way they are taught rhetoric—arises out of a comprehensive version
of reality, bearing important consequences for human behavior.
During the nineteenth century, three such versions appeared,
manifesting themselves in three different rhetorics: the classical,
the psychological-epistemological, and the romantic. At the end of
the century only the second and third remained in force, and in the
twentieth century, a form of the second—current-traditional rhetoric—became dominant.

Beginning in the 1960s, however, current-traditional rhetoric began to be challenged. During the last 20 years or so, composition
teachers have reexamined this approach to teaching students to
write. One of the products has been a mining of the rhetorical tradition in search of alternatives. As a result, rhetorical systems of the
nineteenth century have been reexamined, often with surprising re-

sults. This study would be incomplete without a glance at these developments.

I would like to consider three contemporary approaches to teaching writing that, consciously or unconsciously, reflect rhetorics of the nineteenth century. The three are united in sharing a deliberate attempt to establish a noetic field that is to serve as an alternative to current-traditional rhetoric. At the same time, each is unique in that reality, writer, audience, and language, along with the relationship of each element to the others, are given a distinct formulation. The composing process recommended in each approach is likewise unique because of the differing conceptions governing what can be known, how it can be known, and how it can be communicated. As I hope this history has demonstrated, looking at theories of writing instruction in this way unlocks their implications for behavior. When we teach students to write, we are teaching more than an instrumental skill. We are teaching a mode of conduct, a way of responding to experience. The proponents of the pedagogical theories I will consider are aware of this inevitability. The three theories are the classical, the expressionist, and, for want of a better term, the new rhetoric.[2]

One rhetorical tradition that survived into the nineteenth-century college classroom was the classical, most notably in the work of John Quincy Adams. It was short-lived in the last century, but there have been recent attempts to revive it. Two will be considered here—the separate efforts of Edward P. J. Corbett and Michael Halloran. While these rhetoricians call upon the entire classical heritage, Halloran makes particular reference to American educational practice in the eighteenth century and the uses and decline of classical rhetoric in the nineteenth century. Both are attempting to restore the comprehensiveness of classical rhetoric to the composing process.

The best-known attempt to revive classical rhetoric for writing classes is Edward P. J. Corbett's *Classical Rhetoric for the Modern Student* (1965), and everyone interested in writing instruction must be grateful for his having done so. Corbett has kept before us a model of a comprehensive rhetoric, a reminder of its rich possibilities. He wishes to restore a holistic response to experience in the rhetorical act, encouraging the student to include ethical and aesthetic considerations along with the rational. His approach also returns the notion of probability to rhetoric, taking into account the uncertainty of the issues in rhetoric's domain. In seeking to persuade in this uncertain realm—persuasion once again placed at the center of discourse—the writer must consider the audience as made up of complex individuals who are motivated by emotion as well as reason. While truth is rational, making the true prevail in conduct involves a larger response from both writer and audience. Finally, language is involved at every step of the way in the writing process. While language is conceived as a sign system, expressing reality rather than constitutive of reality, it is important in the subtleties involved in engaging the emotions of the audience and in establishing the character of the writer. It does not simply attempt the expression of rational truth.

Corbett's rhetoric includes provisions for invention, arrangement, and style—guiding the student at every step of the composing act. Thus, invention is provided for, not only in the rational commonplaces, but in the appeals to emotion and from character. Writing, furthermore, involves an interaction between writer and audience, even though this interaction is to establish a truth that exists independent of the rhetorical act itself. The important consideration is that the search for truth is put back into the rhetorical process. Truth is not an original creation since it can always be traced to a prior set of assumptions, but making it prevail is the first concern of the writer. He must then ask basic questions about human values in composing, not simply rely on rational proofs.

Another attempt to reconsider the classical tradition admits that it is "largely incompatible with modern rhetorical and communication theory,"[3] yet looks to it to supply an attractive alternative to current-traditional rhetoric. Michael Halloran has argued eloquently that we have much to learn from classical rhetoric, especially as it was developed in ancient Rome. His main motive for reconsidering this tradition has to do with its emphasis on public discourse as a part of the political decision-making process. The classical tradition insisted that rhetoric deals with public problems, and that "learning in philosophy and literature and the other subjects in college was understood as bearing directly upon the nature of the commonwealth."[4] Halloran sums up the role of classical rhetoric in America prior to its decline in the nineteenth century: "At the end of the 18th century, then, rhetoric at American colleges was the classical art of oral public discourse. It stood very near if not precisely at the center of pedagogical concern. It provided students with an art, and more importantly with copious experience and with a tacit set of values bearing directly on the use of language in managing public affairs."[5] This was lost with the ascent of current-traditional rhetoric, however, especially with its concern for written rather than oral performance. The focus of rhetoric shifted from public discourse and public decisions to private discourse—writing—and aesthetic concerns were introduced as ascendant over all others in rhetoric. The specialization that occurred in American colleges of the nineteenth century further weakened the central place of rhetoric in the experience of students. Finally, colleges in the last century redefined their purpose, away from educating individuals in order that they might serve the community, and toward educating individuals so that they might advance their own professional and economic interests.

From Halloran's point of view, the most deplorable result of this is that we have lost "a rhetoric of citizenship." He would reconsider the classical tradition in rhetoric because it promises to place individuals within a realistic political context, returning them to an awareness of their political possibilities. Halloran is convinced that neither current-traditional rhetoric, nor the new classroom rhetorics challenging it, do this, since none "addresses students as political beings, as members of a body politic in which they have a responsibility to form judgments and influence the judgments of others on public issues. English remains separate from social studies, the arts of discourse from the arts of citizenship."[6]

Halloran wishes to reconsider the classical tradition in rhetoric because it promises to awaken the individual's sense of his political responsibility and power. Expressionist rhetoric attempts to restore to individuals their own identities, their own sense of importance as individuals. As I have indicated earlier, the proponents of this approach see themselves operating within the expressive tradition of Emersonian rhetoric—the tradition articulated in Roberta Ray and others. The focus is on the individual's private struggle to arrive at truth. Thus, although expressionists commonly call upon nineteenth-century romantic rhetoric—the examples of Emerson and Thoreau—they are in my view closer to a Platonic rhetorical tradition in their theory and practice.

In Platonic rhetorical theories, truth is discovered through an internal apprehension, a private vision of a world that transcends the physical. For Plato, the truth can be learned, but not taught. Rhetoric can lead to the discovery of truth, revealing error through dialectical discussion, but it cannot directly communicate it. Plato, does, however, provide a way out of the dilemma. Although the truth transcends language, it can be suggested through using language, with its material referents, in a metaphorical manner. The language of the sensory world can thus be used to suggest what is beyond the senses and beyond language.

This rhetoric is seen in the composition textbooks of William Coles, Jr., Ken Macrorie, James E. Miller and Stephen Judy, and Donald Stewart. These expressionists all stress that truth is conceived as a result of a private vision that must be constantly consulted in writing. They thus emphasize that writing is a personal activity, an expression of a unique voice. The writer must be loyal to his private sense of things, not surrender to the vision of someone else. The teacher cannot train the student to do this. All teachers can do is provide an environment in which the student can teach himself to get in touch with his private vision. This does not mean that these classrooms encourage isolation. Typically, expressionist teachers involve students in continual dialogue with the teacher and with each other. The reason for doing so, however, is not to adapt the message to an audience. The purpose is to get rid of what is untrue to the private vision of the writer, what is, in a word, inauthentic. Dialogue can detect the false, but it is up to the individual to discover the true on his own. The theory of language found in expressionist textbooks is also Platonic. It emphasizes the use of metaphor, explaining that the expression of a fresh, personal vision demands an original use of language. The private apprehension of the real relies on the metaphoric appeal from the known to the unknown, from the public and accessible world of the senses to the inner and privileged immaterial realm, in order to be made available to others. This of course means a theory of organic form, content and form being indistinguishable in the creation of meaning.

The final contemporary development in rhetoric showing elements of nineteenth-century rhetoric is found in a category of thought that I will label, for want of a better term, new rhetoric (although *epistemic rhetoric* would probably serve as well). This category includes a wide diversity of thought emanating from a wide variety of sources. I find the clearest pedagogical manifestation of this rhetoric in the composition textbooks of Peter Elbow, Anne Bert-hoff, and Richard Young, Alton Becker, and Kenneth Pike. I realize that the differences among these three textbooks are considerable. The single feature that brings them together, however, is that they regard rhetoric as epistemic, as a means of arriving at truth, and they place language at the center of this truth-seeking, truth-creating enterprise. In this, they are the rhetorical descendants of Ralph Waldo Emerson and Fred Newton Scott. I hasten to add, however, that I am not claiming any direct influence. Instead, I am asserting that Emerson and Scott were intellectual forebears, putting forth theories of rhetoric that are strikingly similar to contemporary developments. I would like to point out briefly the main points of convergence in the rhetorics of these nineteenth- and twentieth-century thinkers.

These three contemporary classroom rhetorics share with Emerson and Scott the conviction that truth is dynamic and dialectical, the result of a process involving the interaction of opposing elements. Truth is a product of this relation and is created. The basic elements of the dialectic are the elements that make up the communication process—writer (speaker), audience, reality, language. Communication is always basic to the epistemology underlying this rhetoric, because truth is always truth for someone standing in relation to an audience in a linguistically circumscribed situation. The elements of the communication process thus do not simply provide a convenient device for talking about rhetoric. They form the elements that go into the very shaping of knowledge.

Language is at the center of the dialectical interplay between the individual and experience. Truth does not exist apart from language; the difficulty of the writer or speaker is not reduced to finding the appropriate words to communicate knowledge. For these rhetorics, truth is impossible without language since it is language that embodies and generates truth. Language determines the shapes that truth can assume. It does not simply correspond to the "real world." It creates the "real world" by organizing experience, by determining what will be perceived and not perceived, by indicating what has meaning and what is meaningless.

This version of the composing process leads Elbow, Berthoff, and Young, Becker, and Pike to a view of the elements of the writing class that rivals Aristotelian rhetoric in its comprehensiveness. Like the classical rhetoricians, the new rhetoricians see truth as probabilistic, and they provide students with techniques—heuristics—for discovering it, or what might more accurately be called creating it. This does not mean that arrangement and style are regarded as unimportant. Structure and language are a part of the very formation of meaning; they are at the center of the discovery of truth and are not simply the dress of thought. In their classroom practice, these new rhetoricians thus treat in depth all the offices of classical rhetoric that apply to written language—invention, arrangement, and style—and do so by calling upon the best that has been thought and said by their contemporaries.

Before closing this discussion, I should mention a point of contact between new rhetoric and expressionist rhetoric. It is occasionally difficult to distinguish between the two in their theoretical statements and, even more so, in their classroom practice. The emphasis on classroom dialogue in Macrorie and in Miller and Judy, for example, often seems to be an attempt not so much to correct inauthenticity as to create a rhetorical situation for the dialectical discovery of truth. It is as if the Emersonian rhetoric of self-expression tends to become an Emersonian rhetoric of public discourse in the hands of contemporary expressionists.

The three modern rhetorics I have considered—the classical, the expressionist, and the new rhetoric—represent extensions of the best the nineteenth century has to offer. While there is no reason to argue for a simple and direct causal connection between developments so far separated in time, it is heartening to realize that our attempts to improve our classroom performance are including the most promising from the past. On that note, I would like to offer a final word on composition teaching today.

One of the purposes of this study has been to convince writing teachers of their importance. As I mentioned earlier, there have been repeated attempts to abolish the freshman writing course during its brief history of 100 years or so, but none have been successful. I am convinced that this failure is not simply the result of vested interests preserving a useless but profitable enterprise. Freshman writing courses do teach young people to write, if only because their teachers patiently (and sometimes lovingly) pay attention to what a student puts on paper for 30 weeks or so. Most students—especially today's serious, industrious, careerist students—learn what we teach them. For this reason, it is important to be aware of what we are teaching, in all its implications. The way we teach writing behavior, whether we will it or not, causes reverberations in all features of a student's private and social behavior. One obvious reason is that the freshman writing course, despite its low status, is the last vestige of the nineteenth-century collegiate way, almost the only place in a large university where first year students are more than numbers. Beyond that, regardless of one's approach to writing instruction, it is impossible to deny that in teaching students about the way they ought to use language we are teaching them something about how to conduct their lives. We owe it to our students and ourselves to make certain that we are providing the best advice that we can offer. The recent self-examination of our enterprise is ample evidence that we are meeting this responsibility in earnest.

Notes
Bibliography

Notes

1. The Method and the Major Theories

1. See Douglas Ehninger, "On Systems of Rhetoric," *Philosophy and Rhetoric* 1 (1968): 131–44.
2. I am using *noetic* as found in Walter J. Ong, *Rhetoric, Romance, and Technology* (Ithaca, NY: Cornell Univ. Pr., 1971), 317–34.
3. A more recent study that covers much of the same ground is John Michael Wozniak, *English Composition in Eastern Colleges, 1850–1940* (Washington, DC: Univ. Pr. of America, 1978).
4. In discussing Aristotle's philosophy, I am relying on a reading found in Marjorie Grene, *A Portrait of Aristotle* (London: Faber and Faber, 1963). For a different reading of his rhetoric, see William M. A. Grimaldi, *Studies in the Philosophy of Aristotle's Rhetoric* (Wiesbaden: Franz Steiner Verlag, 1972).
5. Chaim Perelman and L. Olbrechts-Tyteca, *The New Rhetoric: A Treatise on Argumentation*, trans. John Wilkinson and Purcell Weaver (Notre Dame: Univ. of Notre Dame Pr., 1969), pt. 1.
6. Douglas Ehninger, "George Campbell and the Revolution in Inventional Theory," *Southern Speech Journal* 15 (1950): 270–76.
7. See Ong, chap. 11; and M. H. Abrams, *The Mirror and the Lamp: Romantic Theory and Critical Tradition* (New York: Oxford Univ. Pr., 1953), chap. 1.

2. The Demise of the Classical Tradition

1. Warren Guthrie, "The Development of Rhetorical Theory in America, 1635–1850," *Speech Monographs* 13 (1946): 22.
2. Ronald F. Reid, "The Boylston Professorship of Rhetoric and Oratory,

1806–1904: A Case Study in Changing Concepts of Rhetoric and Pedagogy," *Quarterly Journal of Speech* 45 (1959): 239.

3. Ibid., 240.

4. Frederick Rudolph, *The American College and University: A History* (New York: Vintage Books, 1962), 26.

5. John Quincy Adams, *Lectures on Rhetoric and Oratory*, 2 vols. (Cambridge, MA: Hilliard and Metcalf, 1810), 1:13–14.

6. Ibid., 14–15.

7. Ibid., 39.

8. Ibid., 40.

9. Kenneth D. Frandsen, "Ward, Adams, and Classical Rhetoric," *Southern Speech Journal* 34 (1968): 110–12.

10. Horace G. Rahskopf, "John Quincy Adams: Speaker and Rhetorician," *Quarterly Journal of Speech* 32 (1946): 438.

11. Ibid.

12. J. Jeffery Auer and Jerald L. Banninga, "The Genesis of John Quincy Adams' Lectures on Rhetoric and Oratory," *Quarterly Journal of Speech* 44 (1963): 119, 132.

13. Cf. Ong, chap. 5.

14. For the history of the American college immediately after the Revolution, see Rudolph, chaps. 1 and 2.

3. The Triumph of Eighteenth-Century Rhetoric

1. George Campbell, *The Philosophy of Rhetoric*, ed. Lloyd F. Bitzer (Carbondale, IL: Southern Illinois Univ. Pr., 1963), 70.

2. Vincent Bevilacqua, "Campbell, Priestley, and Common Sense," *Southern Speech Journal* 30 (1964): 87.

3. Campbell, 1.

4. Ibid.

5. Ibid., 77–78.

6. Ibid., 80.

7. Ibid., 139.

8. Ibid., 190.

9. Ibid., 215.

10. Douglas Ehninger and James Golden, "The Intrinsic Sources of Blair's Popularity," *Southern Speech Journal* 21 (1955): 12–30.

11. Hugh Blair, *Lectures on Rhetoric and Belles Lettres*, ed. Harold F. Harding, 2 vols. (Carbondale, IL: Southern Illinois Univ. Pr., 1965), 2:180.

12. Ibid., 182.

13. For a brief summary of this poetic, see Abrams, 14–21.

14. Blair, 1:41.
15. Ibid., 75.
16. Ibid., 2:312.
17. Ibid., 322.
18. Abrams, 95–96.
19. Blair, 1:184.
20. Ibid., 289.
21. Richard Whately, *Elements of Rhetoric*, ed Douglas Ehninger (Carbondale, IL: Southern Illinois Univ. Pr., 1963), Editor's Introduction, pp. xxviii, xxx.
22. Ibid., 37.
23. Ibid., 25.
24. Ibid., 23.
25. Ibid., 25.
26. Warren Guthrie, "The Development of Rhetorical Theory in America, 1635–1850," *Speech Monographs* 15 (1948): 69.
27. Albert Raymond Kitzhaber, "Rhetoric in American Colleges, 1850–1900" (Ph.D. diss., Univ. of Washington, 1953), 2–3.
28. Rudolph, 63.
29. For a more detailed account, see James A. Berlin, "Transformation of Invention in Nineteenth Century American Rhetoric," *Southern Speech Communication Journal* 46 (1981): 292–304.
30. Elizabeth Flower and Murray G. Murphey, *A History of Philosophy in America*, 2 vols. (New York: G. P. Putnam's Sons, 1977), vol. 1, chap. 4.
31. William Charvat, *The Origins of American Critical Thought, 1810–1835* (1936; reprint, New York: Russell and Russell, 1968), 35.
32. Ibid., 7–26.
33. Guthrie, *Speech Monographs*, 15 (1948): 69.
34. See Ong, chap. 11, for a discusion of this shift in England.

4. American Imitators

1. Kitzhaber, 13–15.
2. Samuel P. Newman, *A Practical System of Rhetoric* (New York: Mark H. Newman, 1846), iii.
3. Ibid., ix.
4. Ibid., 18–19.
5. Ibid., 68.
6. Ibid., 85.
7. Henry Noble Day, *The Art of Discourse* (New York: Charles Scribner's Sons, 1867), 40.

8. Henry Noble Day, *Elements of the Art of Rhetoric* (Hudson, OH: Skinner, 1850), vi.
9. Ibid., viii.
10. Kitzhaber, 159.
11. Rudolph, 132.
12. Ibid., 134.

5. An Alternative Voice: Emerson and Romantic Rhetoric

1. See, for example, Richard Young, "Paradigms and Problems: Needed Research in Rhetorical Invention," in *Research on Composing: Points of Departure*, ed. Charles R. Cooper and Lee Odell (Urbana, IL: National Council of Teachers of English, 1978), 30–33.
2. Robert K. Ray, "The Role of the Orator in the Philosophy of Ralph Waldo Emerson," *Speech Monographs* 41 (1974): 215.
3. Sheldon W. Liebman, "The Development of Emerson's Theory of Rhetoric, 1821–1836," *American Literature* 41 (1969): 178–206.
4. F. O. Matthiessen, *American Renaissance: Art and Expression in the Age of Emerson and Whitman* (London: Oxford Univ. Pr., 1941), 22.
5. The first group includes the following: Ray, "Role of the Orator in the Philosophy of Ralph Waldo Emerson"; Liebman, "Development of Emerson's Theory of Rhetoric, 1821–1836"; Roland F. Lee, "Through Kierkegaard: Toward a Definition of Emerson's Theory of Communication," *ELH* 24 (1957): 229–49; John H. Sloan, "'The Miraculous Uplifting': Emerson's Relationship with His Audience," *Quarterly Journal of Speech* 52 (1966): 10–15. The second group includes the following: William S. Tacey, "Emerson on Eloquence," *Today's Speech* 6 (1958): 23–27; Herbert A. Wichelns, "Ralph Waldo Emerson," in *A History and Criticism of American Public Address*, ed. William Norwood Brigance (New York: Russell and Russell, 1960).
6. For a summary of this tradition, see Lawrence W. Rosenfield, "An Autopsy of the Rhetorical Tradition," in *The Prospect of Rhetoric*, ed. Lloyd F. Bitzer and Edwin Black (Englewood Cliffs, NJ: Prentice-Hall, 1971), 64–77.
7. Robert Cushman, *Therapeia* (Chapel Hill: Univ. of North Carolina Pr., 1958), 213.
8. Ray, 218.
9. Ibid., 219.
10. Ibid., 223.
11. Ibid., 224.
12. James A. Berlin, "Contemporary Composition: The Major Pedagogical Theories," *College English* 44 (1982): 771–73.

13. Liebman, 96.
14. References in Emerson are to *The Complete Works of Ralph Waldo Emerson* (Boston: Houghton Mifflin, 1903, 1:63.
15. Ibid., 1:64.
16. Ibid., 50.
17. Ibid., 25.
18. Ibid., 29.
19. Ibid., 26.
20. Ibid., 30–31.
21. Ibid., 27–28.
22. Ibid., 32.
23. Richard M. Weaver, "The *Phaedrus* and the Nature of Rhetoric," in *The Province of Rhetoric*, ed Joseph Schwartz and John A. Rycenga (New York: Ronald Press, 1965), 323.
24. Emerson, *Complete Works*, 8:115.
25. Ibid., 112.
26. Ibid., 7:61.
27. Ibid., 8:118.
28. Ibid., 7:62.
29. Ibid.
30. Ibid., 1:29.
31. Ibid., 7:64.
32. Ibid., 8:130.
33. Ibid., 7:93.
34. Ibid., 89.
35. Ibid., 93.
36. Ibid., 98.
37. Ibid., 94.
38. Ibid., 90.
39. Ibid., 91.
40. Ibid., 8:124.
41. Ibid., 129.
42. Ibid., 7:93.
43. Ibid., 96–97.
44. Ibid., 1:29–30.
45. Ibid., 30.
46. Ibid., 7:92.
47. Ibid., 95.
48. *The Journals and Miscellaneous Notebooks of Ralph Waldo Emerson*, vol. 5, ed. Merton W. Sealts, Jr. (Cambridge, MA: Harvard Univ. Pr., 1965), 223.
49. Emerson, *Complete Works*, 7:65.
50. Ibid., 63.

51. Sloan, 12.
52. Emerson, *Complete Works*, 7:84.
53. Ibid., 8:125.
54. Ibid., 7:66.
55. Ibid., 8:115–116.
56. Ibid., 7:97.
57. Ibid., 8:132–33.
58. Rudolph, 218.

6. Current-Traditional Rhetoric

1. Rudolph, 274–75.
2. Ibid., 294.
3. Ibid., 281.
4. Kitzhaber, 72–73.
5. Ibid., 71–79. It should be heartening to today's composition teachers to know that of the students writing the entrance exam at Harvard in 1892, 47% "passed unsatisfactorily," 2% passed "with credit," and 20% failed altogether. These results were not atypical for the time.
6. See Kitzhaber, 156–68; and Ernest Earl Ettlich, "Theories of Invention in Late Nineteenth Century American Rhetoric," *Western Speech Journal* 30 (1966): 233–41.
7. Adams Sherman Hill, *The Principles of Rhetoric and Their Application* (New York: American Book Co., 1878), vi.
8. Kitzhaber, 222; Robert J. Connors, "The Rise and Fall of the Modes of Discourse," *College Composition and Communication* 32 (1981): 444–55.
9. John Franklin Genung, *The Practical Elements of Rhetoric* (Amherst, MA: J. E. Williams, 1885).
10. Ibid., 326.
11. Ibid., 348.
12. Ibid., 355.
13. Ibid., 383.
14. Ibid., 408.
15. Ibid., 3.
16. Ibid., 449.
17. Hill, 248.
18. Ibid., 300.
19. Ibid., 326.
20. Ibid., 386.
21. Ibid., 387.
22. Kitzhaber, 219.

23. John Franklin Genung, *A Study of Rhetoric in the College Course* (Boston: D. C. Heath and Co., 1887), 26–28.
24. Kitzhaber, 242–64.
25. A. D. Hepburn, *Manual of English Rhetoric* (Cincinnati, OH: Van Antwerp, Bragg and Co., 1875), 147.
26. Kitzhaber, 184–90.
27. Barrett Wendell, *English Composition* (New York: Charles Scribner's Sons, 1891), 29.
28. Later, this order was reversed, perhaps in recognition that decisions about the parts must be made with reference to the whole.
29. Wendell, vii.
30. Blair, 1:184.
31. Kitzhaber, 269–70.
32. Ibid., 273.
33. Ong, chap. 11.
34. Wallace Douglas, "Rhetoric for the Meritocracy," in Richard Ohmann, *English in America: A Radical View of the Profession* (New York: Oxford Univ. Pr., 1976), 97–132.
35. Kitzhaber, 299–311.
36. Genung, *Study of Rhetoric in the College Course*, 10.
37. Wendell, 1–4.
38. Kitzhaber, 331.
39. See, for example, Genung, *Practical Elements of Rhetoric*, 248–326; and Alphonso G. Newcomer, *A Practical Course in English Composition* (Boston: Ginn and Co., 1893), 1–65.
40. Cf. Richard Ohmann, *English in America: A Radical View of the Profession* (New York: Oxford Univ. Pr., 1976), chaps. 6–7.

7. An Alternative Voice: Fred Newton Scott

1. See Donald C. Stewart, "The Barnyard Goose, History, and Fred Newton Scott," *English Journal* 67 (1978): 14–17; and Donald C. Stewart, "Rediscovering Fred Newton Scott," *College English* 40 (1979): 539–47.
2. Kitzhaber, 204–5, 209–10.
3. Cf. Donald J. Butler, *Four Philosophies and Their Practice in Education and Religion* (New York: Harper and Row, 1968), 382–94.
4. Fred Newton Scott, "English Composition as a Mode of Behavior," *English Journal* 11 (1922): 467.
5. Ibid., 468.
6. Ibid., 467.
7. Ibid., 468.

8. Ibid., 470.
9. Ibid., 470–71.
10. Ibid., 472.
11. Kitzhaber, 282.
12. Fred Newton Scott, "The Two Ideals of Composition Teaching," in *The Standard of American Speech and Other Papers* (New York: Allyn and Bacon, 1926), 36.
13. Ibid., 43.
14. Ibid., 40.
15. Fred Newton Scott, "The Standard of American Speech," *English Journal* 6 (1917): 9.
16. Arthur N. Applebee, *Tradition and Reform in the Teaching of English* (Urbana, IL: National Council of Teachers of English, 1974), 47–48.
17. Fred Newton Scott and Joseph Villiers Denney, *Elementary English Composition* (Boston: Allyn and Bacon, 1900), iii.
18. Ibid., iv.
19. From Joseph V. Denney, *Two Problems in Composition-Teaching*, printed as no. 3 in *Contributions to Rhetorical Theory*, ed. Fred Newton Scott (Ann Arbor, MI: n.d.). Quoted in Kitzhaber, 176.
20. Kitzhaber, 285.
21. From Gertrude Buck, *The Metaphor—A Study in the Psychology of Rhetoric*, printed as no. 5 in *Contributions to Rhetorical Theory*, ed. Fred Newton Scott (Ann Arbor, MI: n.p., 1899), 35. Quoted in Kitzhaber, 287.
22. Fred Newton Scott and Joseph Villiers Denney, *Composition-Rhetoric, Designed for Use in Secondary Schools* (Boston, Allyn and Bacon, 1897), iv.
23. Kenneth J. Kantor, "Creative Expression in the English Curriculum: A Historical Perspective," *Research in Teaching English* 9 (1975): 5–29.

8. Postscript on the Present

1. Leonard Greenbaum, "The Tradition of Complaint," *College English* 31 (1969): 174–87.
2. For a more detailed discussion, see Berlin, "Contemporary Composition: The Major Pedagogical Theories," 765–77.
3. Michael Halloran, "Tradition and Theory in Rhetoric," *Quarterly Journal of Speech* 62 (1976): 234.
4. Michael Halloran, "Rhetoric in the American College Curriculum: The Decline of Public Discourse," *PRE/TEXT* 3 (1982): 256.
5. Ibid., 257.
6. Ibid., 263.

Bibliography

Primary Sources

Adams, John Quincy. *Lectures on Rhetoric and Oratory, Delivered to the Classes of Senior and Junior Sophisters in Harvard University*. 2 vols. Cambridge, MA: Hilliard and Metcalf, 1810.

Bain, Alexander. *Autobiography*. London: Longmans, Green and Co., 1904.

————. *Education as a Science*. London: C. Kegan Paul and Co., 1879.

————. *English Composition and Rhetoric: A Manual*. London: Longmans, Green and Co., 1866.

————. *On Teaching English*. London: Longmans, Green and Co., 1887.

————. *Practical Essays*. London: Longmans, Green and Co., 1884.

————. "Rhetoric." In *Information for the People*, edited by W. and R. Chambers, 2:689–704. Edinburgh: W. and R. Chambers, 1849.

Baldwin, Charles Sears. *A College Manual of Rhetoric*. New York: Longmans, Green and Co., 1902.

————. "The College Teaching of Rhetoric." *Educational Review* 48 (1914): 1–20.

————. *Composition, Oral and Written*. New York: Longmans, Green and Co., 1909.

————. *The Expository Paragraph and Sentence. An Elementary Manual of Composition*. New York: Longmans, Green and Co., 1897.

————. "Freshman English." *Educational Review* 32 (1906): 385–94, 485–99.

————. "The Value of the Office-Hour in the Teaching of Rhetoric." *Educational Review* 8 (1894): 290–93.

————. *Writing and Speaking, a Text-Book of Rhetoric*. New York: Longmans, Green and Co., 1909.

Barbour, F. A. "History of English Grammar Teaching." *Educational Review* 12 (1896): 487–507.

————. "The Psychology of the Diagram," *School Review* 5 (1897): 240–42.

Bascom, John. *Philosophy of Rhetoric*. Boston: Crosby and Ainsworth, 1866.

Bates, Arlo. *Talks on Writing English, First Series*. Boston: Houghton Mifflin, 1896.

————. *Talks on Writing English, Second Series*. Boston: Houghton Mifflin, 1901.

Blair, Hugh. *Lectures on Rhetoric and Belles Lettres*. Edited by Harold F. Harding. 2 vols. Carbondale, IL: Southern Illinois Univ. Pr., 1965.

Boyd, James R. *Elements of English Composition, Grammatical, Rhetorical, Logical, and Practical. Prepared for Academies and Schools*. New York: A. S. Barnes and Burr, 1860.

————. *Elements of Logic: On the Basis of Lectures by William Barron*. New York: A. S. Barnes, 1856.

————. *Elements of Rhetoric and Literary Criticism*. New York: Harper and Brothers, 1844.

Brewster, William T. *English Composition and Style*. New York: Century Co., 1912.

————. *Studies in Structure and Style (Based on Seven Modern English Essays)*, with an introduction by G. R. Carpenter. New York: Macmillan Co., 1896.

Buck, Gertrude. *A Course in Argumentative Writing*. New York: Henry Holt and Co., 1899.

————. *Figures of Rhetoric; A Psychological Study*. (*Contributions to Rhetorical Theory*, no. 1). Ann Arbor, MI: n.p., 1895.

————. "Make-Believe Grammar." *School Review* 17 (1909): 21–23.

————. *The Metaphor—A Study in the Psychology of Rhetoric*. (*Contributions to Rhetorical Theory*, no. 5, edited by Fred Newton Scott). Ann Arbor, MI: n.p., 1899.

————. "The Present Status of Rhetorical Theory." *Modern Language Notes* 15 (1900): 167–74.

————. "The Psychological Significance of the Parts of Speech." *Education* 18 (1898): 269–77.

————. "The Psychology of the Diagram." *School Review* 5 (1897): 470–72.

————. "Recent Tendencies in the Teaching of English Composition." *Educational Review* 22 (1901): 371–82.

————. "The Sentence-Diagram." *Educational Review* 13 (1897): 250–60.

————. *The Social Criticism of Literature.* New Haven, CT: Yale Univ. Pr., 1916.

————. "What Does 'Rhetoric' Mean?" *Educational Review* 22 (1901): 197–200.

Buck, Gertrude, and Kristine Mann. *A Handbook of Argumentation and Debating.* Orange, NJ: The Orange Chronicle, 1906.

Buck, Gertrude, and Elisabeth Woodbridge Morris. *A Course in Expository Writing.* New York: Henry Holt and Co., 1899.

————. *A Course in Narrative Writing.* New York: Henry Holt and Co., 1906.

Cairns, William B. *The Forms of Discourse.* Boston: Ginn and Co., 1896.

————. *Introduction to Rhetoric.* Boston: Ginn and Co., 1899.

Campbell, George. *The Philosophy of Rhetoric.* Edited by Lloyd F. Bitzer. Carbondale, IL: Southern Illinois Univ. Pr., 1963.

Carpenter, George R. *Elements of Rhetoric and English Composition, First and Second High School Courses.* New York: Macmillan Co., 1900.

————. "English Composition in Colleges." *Educational Review* 4 (1892): 438–46.

————. *Exercises in Rhetoric and English Composition Advanced Course.* Boston: Willard Small, 1882.

————. *Rhetoric and English Composition.* New York: Macmillan Co., 1906.

Carpenter, George R., Franklin T. Baker, and Fred N. Scott. *The Teaching of English in the Elementary and the Secondary School.* New York: Longmans, Green and Co., 1903.

Clark, J. Scott. "The Art of English Composition." *Academy* 4 (1889): 369–84.

————. *A Practical Rhetoric, for Instruction in English Composition and Revision in Colleges and Intermediate Schools.* New York: Henry Holt and Co., 1886.

Clark, S. H., and F. M. Blanchard. *Practical Public Speaking.* New York: Charles Scribner's Sons, 1899.

Day, Henry Noble. *The Art of Discourse*. New York: Charles Scribner's Sons, 1867.

————. *Art of Elocution*. New Haven, CT: A. H. Maltby, 1844.

————. *Elements of Logic*. New York: Charles Scribner's Sons, 1867.

————. *Elements of the Art of Rhetoric*. Hudson, OH: Skinner, 1850.

————. *Grammatical Synthesis. The Art of English Composition*. New York: Charles Scribner's Sons, 1867.

————. *Logical Praxis*. New Haven, CT: C. C. Chatfield, 1872.

————. *Rhetorical Praxis*. Cincinnati, OH: Moore, Wilstach, Keys, and Co., 1861.

————. *The Science of Aesthetics*. New Haven, CT: C. C. Chatfield, 1872.

————. *The Science of Thought*. New York: Ivison, Blakeman, Taylor, and Co., 1886.

Demille, James. *The Elements of Rhetoric*. New York: Harper and Brothers, 1878.

Denney, Joseph V. *Two Problems in Composition-Teaching*. (*Contributions to Rhetorical Theory*, no. 3, edited by Fred Newton Scott). Ann Arbor, MI: n.d.

Denney, Joseph V., Carsons Duncan, and Frank C. McKinney. *Argumentation and Debate*. New York: American Book Co., 1910.

Emerson, Ralph Waldo. *The Complete Works of Ralph Waldo Emerson*. 12 vols. Boston: Houghton Mifflin, 1903.

————. *The Journals and Miscellaneous Notebooks of Ralph Waldo Emerson*. Vol. 5. Edited by Merton M. Sealts, Jr. Cambridge, MA: Harvard Univ. Pr., 1965.

Genung, John Franklin. *Handbook of Rhetorical Analysis: Studies in Style and Invention*. Boston: Ginn and Co., 1888.

————. *Outlines of Rhetoric*. Boston: Ginn and Co., 1893.

————. *The Practical Elements of Rhetoric*. Amherst, MA: J. E. Williams, 1885.

————. *A Study of Rhetoric in the College Course*. Boston: D. C. Heath and Co., 1887.

————. *The Working Principles of Rhetoric*. Boston: Ginn and Co., 1900.

Hart, James Morgan. *A Handbook of Composition and Rhetoric*. Philadelphia: Eldredge and Brother, 1894.

————. "On the Approaches to the English Language." *Presbyterian Quarterly and Princeton Review* 3 (1874): 434–56.

Hart, John S. *First Lessons in Composition*. Philadelphia: Eldredge and Brother, 1871.

———. *A Manual of Composition and Rhetoric*. Philadelphia: Eldredge and Brother, 1870.

Haven, E. O. *Rhetoric: A Textbook*. New York: Harper and Brothers, 1869.

Hepburn, A. D. *Manual of English Rhetoric*. Cincinnati, OH: Van Antwerp, Bragg and Co., 1875.

Hill, Adams Sherman. *Beginnings of Rhetoric and Composition*. New York: American Book Co., 1902.

———. "English in Our Colleges." *Scribner's Magazine* 1 (1887): 507–12.

———. *The Foundations of Rhetoric*. New York: Harper and Brothers, 1892.

———. *Our English*. New York: Harper and Brothers, 1888.

———. *The Principles of Rhetoric and Their Application*. New York: American Book Co., 1878.

Hill, Adams Sherman, L. B. R. Briggs, and B. S. Hurlbut. *Twenty Years of School and College English*. Cambridge, MA: Harvard Univ. Pr., 1896.

Hill, David J. *The Elements of Rhetoric and Composition*. New York: Sheldon and Co., 1878.

———. *The Science of Rhetoric*. New York: Sheldon and Co., 1877.

Hinsdale, B. A. *Teaching the Language Arts*. New York: D. Appleton and Co., 1896.

Hope, M. B. *The Princeton Text-Book in Rhetoric*. Princeton, NJ: John T. Robinson, 1859.

Huffcutt, E. W. *English in the Preparatory Schools*. Boston: D. C. Heath and Co., 1887.

Hunt, Theodore W. "The Place of English in the College Curriculum." In *Modern Language Association Publications*, vol. 1, Baltimore, 1886.

———. *The Principles of Written Discourse*. New York: A. C. Armstrong and Son, 1884.

———. "Rhetorical Science." *Presbyterian Quarterly and Princeton Review* 3 (1874): 660–78.

———. *Studies in Literature and Style*. New York: A. C. Armstrong and Son, 1890.

———. "The Study of English in American Colleges." *Educational Review* 12 (1896): 140–50.

Kellogg, Brainerd, "On Teaching English." *School Review* 1 (1893): 96–105, 152–62.

————. *A Text-Book on Rhetoric.* New York: Clark and Maynard, 1880.

Lewis, Edwin H. *The History of the English Paragraph.* Chicago: Univ. of Chicago Pr., 1894.

Newcomer, Alphonso G. *Elements of Rhetoric: A Course in Plain Prose Composition.* New York: Henry Holt and Co., 1898.

————. *A Practical Course in English Composition.* Boston: Ginn and Co., 1893.

Newman, Samuel P. *A Lecture on a Practical Method of Teaching Rhetoric.* Boston: Hilliard, Little, and Wilkins, 1830.

————. *A Practical System of Rhetoric.* New York: Mark H. Newman, 1846. (First published Portland, Maine, 1827).

Parker, Richard Green. *Aids to English Composition, Prepared for Students of All Grades.* New York: Harper and Brothers, 1845.

Quackenbos, George Payn. *Advanced Course of Composition and Rhetoric.* New York: D. Appleton and Co., 1854.

————. *First Lessons in Composition.* New York: D. Appleton and Co., 1851.

Quackenbos, John Duncan. *Practical Rhetoric.* New York: American Book Co., 1896.

Reed, Alonzo, and Brainerd Kellogg. *Higher Lessons in English.* New York: Clark and Maynard, 1878.

Scott, Fred Newton. "English Composition as a Mode of Behavior." *English Journal* 11 (1922): 463–73.

————. *The Principles of Style.* Ann Arbor, MI: Register Publishing Co., 1890.

————. *References on the Teaching of Rhetoric and Composition.* (*Contributions to Rhetorical Theory*, no. 4, edited by Fred Newton Scott). N.p., n.d.

————. "The Report on College-Entrance Requirements in English," *Educational Review* 20 (1900), 289–94.

————. *The Standard of American Speech and Other Papers.* New York: Allyn and Bacon, 1926.

————. "What the West Wants in Preparatory English." *School Review* 17 (1909): 10–20.

Scott, Fred Newton, and Gertrude Buck. *A Brief English Grammar.* Chicago: Scott, Foresman and Co., 1905.

Scott, Fred Newton, and Joseph Villiers Denney. *Composition-Literature.* Boston: Allyn and Bacon, 1902.

———. *Composition-Rhetoric, Designed for Use in Secondary Schools.* Boston: Allyn and Bacon, 1897.

———. *Elementary English Composition.* Boston: Allyn and Bacon, 1900.

———. *The New Composition-Rhetoric.* Boston: Allyn and Bacon, 1911.

———. *Paragraph-Writing.* Ann Arbor, MI: Register Publishing Co., 1891.

Sherman, L. A. *Analytics of Literature: A Manual for the Objective Study of English Prose and Poetry.* Boston: Ginn and Co., 1893.

———. *Elements of Literature and Composition, a Manual for Schools.* Lincoln, NE: University Publishing Co., 1908.

———. "English and English Literature in the College." *Educational Review* 10 (1895): 42–56.

Thurber, Samuel. "An Address to Teachers of English." *Education* 18 (1898): 515–26.

———. "English Work in the Secondary Schools." *School Review* 1 (1893): 650–55.

———. "Five Axioms of Composition Teaching." *School Review* 5 (1897): 7–17.

Wendell, Barrett. *English Composition.* New York: Charles Scribner's Sons, 1891.

———. "English Work in the Second Schools." *School Review* 1 (1893): 638–50.

Whately, Richard. *Elements of Logic.* London: Fellowes, 1826.

———. *Elements of Rhetoric.* Edited by Douglas Ehninger. Carbondale, IL: Southern Illinois Univ. Pr., 1963.

Witherspoon, John. *Lectures on Moral Philosophy and Eloquence.* Woodward's 3d ed. Philadelphia: William W. Woodward, 1810. The two earlier editions are manuscripts.

Secondary Sources

Abrams, M. H. *The Mirror and the Lamp: Romantic Theory and Critical Tradition.* New York: Oxford Univ. Pr., 1953.

Allen, R. R. "The Rhetoric of John Franklin Genung." *Speech Teacher* 12 (1963): 238–41.

Anderson, Dorothy I. "Edward T. Channing's Definition of Rhetoric." *Speech Monographs* 14 (1947): 81–92.

———. "Edward T. Channing's Teaching of Rhetoric." *Speech Monographs* 16 (1949): 69–81.

Applebee, Arthur N. *Tradition and Reform in the Teaching of English.* Urbana, IL: National Council of Teachers of English, 1974.

Auer, J. Jefferey, and Jerald L. Banninga, "The Genesis of John Quincy Adams' Lectures on Rhetoric and Oratory." *Quarterly Journal of Speech* 44 (1963): 119–32.

Banninga, Jerald L. "John Quincy Adams as a Contemporary Critic." *Central States Speech Journal* 16 (1965): 173–78.

Berlin, James A. "Contemporary Composition: The Major Pedagogical Theories," *College English* 44 (1982): 765–77.

————. "The Transformation of Invention in Nineteenth Century American Rhetoric." *Southern Speech Communication Journal* 46 (1981): 292–304.

Berlin, James A., and Robert P. Inkster. "Current-Traditional Rhetoric: Paradigm and Practice." *Freshman English News* 8 (1980): 1–4, 13–14.

Bevilacqua, Vincent. "Campbell, Priestley, and Common Sense." *Southern Speech Journal* 30 (1964): 79–97.

Butler, Donald J. *Four Philosophies and Their Practice in Education and Religion.* New York: Harper and Row, 1968.

Charvat, William. *The Origins of American Critical Thought, 1810–1835.* 1936. Reprint. New York: Russell and Russell, 1968.

Connors, Robert J. "The Rise and Fall of the Modes of Discourse." *College Composition and Communication* 32 (1981): 444–55.

————. "Static Abstractions and Composition." *Freshman English News* 12 (1983): 1–12.

Corbett, Edward P. J. "A Survey of Rhetoric." In his *Classical Rhetoric for the Modern Student.* New York: Oxford Univ. Pr., 1965.

Culp, Ralph B. "Charles Sears Baldwin." *Speech Teacher* 10 (1961): 169–75.

Cushman, Robert. *Therapeia.* Chapel Hill: Univ. of North Carolina Pr., 1958.

Douglas, Wallace. "Barrett Wendell and the Contradictions of Composition." *Arizona English Bulletin* 16, no. 2 (1974): 182–90.

————. "Rhetoric for the Meritocracy." In Richard Ohmann, *English in America: A Radical View of the Profesion.* New York: Oxford Univ. Pr., 1976.

————. "Why Know Our History." *English Journal* 68, no. 4 (1979): 16–21.

Edney, Clarence W. "English Sources of Rhetorical Theory in Nineteenth-Century America." In *History of Speech Education in America: Background Studies,* edited by Karl R. Wallace, 80–104. New York: Appleton-Century-Crofts, 1954.

Ehninger, Douglas. "Campbell, Blair, and Whately: Old Friends in a New Light." *Western Speech Journal* 19 (1955): 263–69.

———. "Campbell, Blair, and Whately Revisited." *Southern Speech Journal* 28 (1963): 169–82.

———. "George Campbell and the Revolution in Inventional Theory." *Southern Speech Journal* 15 (1950): 270–76.

———. "On Systems of Rhetoric." *Philosophy and Rhetoric* 1 (1968): 131–44.

Ehninger, Douglas, and James Golden. "The Intrinsic Sources of Blair's Popularity." *Southern Speech Journal* 21 (1955): 12–30.

Ettlich, Ernest Earl. "John Franklin Genung and the Nineteenth Century Definition of Rhetoric." *Central States Speech Journal* 17 (1966): 283–88.

———. "Theories of Invention in Late Nineteenth Century American Rhetoric." *Western Speech Journal* 30 (1966): 233–41.

Faules, Don. "Joseph Villiers Denney: English Scholar and Contributor in the Emergence of Speech Theory." *Speech Teacher* 12 (1963): 105–9.

Flower, Elizabeth, and Murray G. Murphey. *A History of Philosophy in America.* 2 vols. New York: G. P. Putnam's Sons, 1977.

Frandsen, Kenneth D. "Ward, Adams, and Classical Rhetoric." *Southern Speech Journal* 34 (1968): 108–15.

Greenbaum, Leonard. "The Tradition of Complaint." *College English* 31 (1969): 174–87.

Grene, Marjorie. *A Portrait of Aristotle.* London: Faber and Faber, 1963.

Grimaldi, William M. A. *Studies in the Philosophy of Artistotle's Rhetoric.* Wiesbaden: Franz Steiner Verlag, 1972.

Guthrie, Warren. "The Development of Rhetorical Theory in America, 1636–1850." *Speech Monographs* 13 (1946): 14–22; 14 (1947): 38–54; 15 (1948): 61–71; 16 (1949): 98–113; 18 (1951): 17–30.

Halloran, Michael. "Rhetoric in the American College Curriculum: The Decline of Public Discourse." *PRE/TEXT* 3 (1982): 245–69.

———. "Tradition and Theory in Rhetoric." *Quarterly Journal of Speech* 62 (1976): 234–41.

Harrington, Elbert. "Rhetoric and the Scientific Method of Inquiry." *University of Colorado Studies, Series in Language and Literature* 1 (Dec. 1948): 1–64.

Hochmuth, Marie, and Richard Murphy. "Rhetorical and Elocutionary Training in Nineteenth-Century Colleges." In *History of Speech Education in America: Background Studies*, edited by Karl R. Wallace, 153–177. New York: Appleton-Century-Crofts, 1954.

Hoshor, John P. "American Contributions to Rhetorical Theory and Homiletics." In *History of Speech Education in America: Background Studies*, edited by Karl L. Wallace, 129–152. New York: Appleton-Century-Crofts, 1954.

Howell, Wilbur Samuel. *Eighteenth-Century British Logic and Rhetoric*. Princeton, NJ: Princeton Univ. Pr., 1971.

Kantor, Kenneth J. "Creative Expression in the English Curriculum: A Historical Perspective." *Research in Teaching English* 9 (1975): 5–29.

Kitzhaber, Albert R. *A Bibliography of Rhetoric in American Colleges, 1850–1900*. Denver, CO: Bibliographic Center for Research, Denver Public Library, 1954.

―――. "Rhetoric in American Colleges, 1850–1900." Ph.D., Univ. of Washington, 1953.

Lee, Roland F. "Through Kierkegaard: Toward a Definition of Emerson's Theory of Communication." *ELH* 24 (1957): 229–49.

Lewis, Edwin. *The History of the English Paragraph*. Chicago: Univ. of Chicago Pr., 1894.

Liebman, Sheldon W. "The Development of Emerson's Theory of Rhetoric, 1821–1836." *American Literature* 41 (1969): 178–206.

Matthiessen, F. O. *American Renaissance: Art and Expression in the Age of Emerson and Whitman*. London: Oxford Univ. Pr., 1941.

Ohmann, Richard. *English in America: A Radical View of the Profession*. New York: Oxford Univ. Pr., 1976.

Ong, Walter J. *Rhetoric, Romance, and Technology*. Ithaca, NY: Cornell Univ. Pr., 1971.

Parker, William Riley. "Where do English Departments Come From?" *College English* 28 (1967): 339–51.

Perelman, Chaim, and L. Olbrechts-Tyteca. *The New Rhetoric: A Treatise on Argumentation*. Translated by John Wilkinson and Purcell Weaver. Notre Dame: Univ. of Notre Dame Pr., 1969.

Rahskopf, Horace G. "John Quincy Adams: Speaker and Rhetorician." *Quarterly Journal of Speech* 32 (1946): 435–41.

Ray, Roberta K. "The Role of the Orator in the Philosophy of Ralph Waldo Emerson." *Speech Monographs* 41 (1974): 215–25.

Reid, Ronald F. "The Boylston Professorship of Rhetoric and Oratory, 1806–1904: A Case Study in Changing Concepts of Rhetoric and Pedagogy." *Quarterly Journal of Speech* 45 (1959): 239–57.

Reports of the Visiting Committees of the Board of Overseers of Harvard College. Cambridge, MA: 1902.

Ried, Paul Eugene. "The Boylston Chair of Rhetoric and Oratory." *Western Speech Journal* 24 (1960): 83–88.

————. "Francis J. Child: The Fourth Boylston Professor of Rhetoric and Oratory." *Quarterly Journal of Speech* 55 (1969): 268–75.

————. "Joseph McKean: The Second Boylston Professor of Rhetoric and Oratory." *Quarterly Journal of Speech* 46 (1960): 419–24.

Robb, Mary Margaret. *Oral Interpretation of Literature in American Colleges and Universities.* New York: H. W. Wilson Co., 1941.

Robinson, H. Alan. *Reading and Writing Instruction in the United States: Historical Trends.* International Reading Association and ERIC Clearinghouse on Reading and Communications Skills, 1977.

Rodgers, Paul C., Jr. "Alexander Bain and the Rise of the Organic Paragraph." *Quarterly Journal of Speech* 51 (1965): 399–408.

Rosenfield, Lawrence W. "An Autopsy of the Rhetorical Tradition." In *The Prospect of Rhetoric,* edited by Lloyd F. Bitzer and Edwin Black. Englewood Cliffs, NJ: Prentice-Hall, 1971.

Rousseau, L. G. "The Rhetorical Principles of Cicero and Adams." *Quarterly Journal of Speech* 2 (1916): 397–410.

Rudolph, Frederick. *The American College and University: A History.* New York: Vintage Books, 1962.

Sandford, William P. *English Theories of Public Address, 1530–1828.* Columbus, OH: Harold L. Hedrick, 1965.

Self, Robert T. *Barrett Wendell.* Boston: Twayne Publishers, 1975.

Shearer, Ned A. "Alexander Bain and the Genesis of Paragraph Theory." *Quarterly Journal of Speech* 58 (1972): 408–17.

————. "Alexander Bain and the Teaching of Rhetoric." *Central States Speech Journal* 23 (1972): 36–43.

————. "Psychology as Foundation to Rhetoric: Alexander Bain and Association Psychology's Relation to Rhetorical Theory." *Western Speech Journal* 35 (1971): 162–68.

Sloan, Douglas. *The Scottish Enlightenment and the American College Ideal.* New York: Teachers College Pr., 1971.

Sloan, John H. "'The Miraculous Uplifting': Emerson's Relationship with His Audience." *Quarterly Journal of Speech* 52 (1966): 10–15.

Stewart, Donald C. "The Barnyard Goose, History, and Fred Newton Scott." *English Journal* 67 (1978): 14–17.

————. "Rediscovering Fred Newton Scott." *College English* 40 (1979): 539–47.

Tacey, William S. "Emerson on Eloquence." *Today's Speech* 6 (1958): 23–27.

Thonssen, Lester, A. Craig Baird, and Waldo W. Braden. *Speech Criticism*. 2d ed. New York: Ronald Press, 1970.

Wallace, Karl R., ed. *History of Speech Education in America: Background Studies*. New York: Appleton-Century-Crofts, 1954.

Weaver, Richard M. "The *Phaedrus* and the Nature of Rhetoric." In *The Province of Rhetoric*, edited by Joseph Schwartz and John A. Rycenga. New York: Ronald Press, 1965.

Wichelns, Herbert A. "Ralph Waldo Emerson." In *A History and Criticism of American Public Address*, edited by William Norwood Brigance. New York: Russell and Russell, 1960.

Wilson, Paul B. "John Witherspoon's Theory and Practice of Public Speaking." *Speech Monographs* 16 (1949): 272–89.

Windhover, Ruth. "Literature in the Nineteenth Century." *English Journal* 68, no. 4 (1979): 28–33.

Wozniak, John Michael. *English Composition in Eastern Colleges, 1850–1940*. Washington, DC: Univ. Pr. of Ameica, 1978.

Young, Richard. "Paradigms and Problems: Needed Research in Rhetorical Invention." In *Research on Composing: Points of Departure*, edited by Charles R. Cooper and Lee Odell. Urbana, IL: National Council of Teachers of English, 1978.